Palgrave Studies in Economic History

Series Editor
Kent Deng
London School of Economics
London, UK

Palgrave Studies in Economic History is designed to illuminate and enrich our understanding of economies and economic phenomena of the past. The series covers a vast range of topics including financial history, labour history, development economics, commercialisation, urbanisation, industrialisation, modernisation, globalisation, and changes in world economic orders.

More information about this series at
http://www.palgrave.com/gp/series/14632

Benny Carlson

Swedish Economists in the 1930s Debate on Economic Planning

palgrave
macmillan

Benny Carlson
Lund University
Lund, Sweden

Palgrave Studies in Economic History
ISBN 978-3-030-03699-7   ISBN 978-3-030-03700-0   (eBook)
https://doi.org/10.1007/978-3-030-03700-0

Library of Congress Control Number: 2018961180

Cover illustration: © nemesis2207/Fotolia.co.uk

This Palgrave Pivot imprint is published by the registered company Springer Nature Switzerland AG
The registered company address is: Gewerbestrasse 11, 6330 Cham, Switzerland

To the memory of Margareta

Contents

1

Introduction

Abstract In times of crisis, demand for government action in general and economic planning in particular is sure to surge. The interwar era is a classic example. After the outbreak of the Great Depression in 1929, demand for planning—in contrast to capitalist market "anarchy"—was voiced in many quarters. And not only voiced. The 1930s was an era of populism, nationalism, protectionism, government intervention and attempts to create planned economies. With the Great Recession of 2008, structural change due to globalization, waves of migration and impending climate change, a new era of populism, nationalism, protectionism and demand for planning has begun. The ambition of this book is to survey the arguments for and against economic planning as they were put forward by leading Swedish economists in the 1930s and to put these arguments into a context of events and inspirational sources. Developments in Sweden were, according to political scientist Leif Lewin's classic exposition of the debate on economic planning in Sweden, "something extraordinary also from an international perspective".

Keywords Economic planning · 1930s · Great Depression · Great Recession · Swedish economists

© The Author(s) 2018
B. Carlson, *Swedish Economists in the 1930s Debate on Economic Planning*, Palgrave Studies in Economic History,
https://doi.org/10.1007/978-3-030-03700-0_1

1

Why, When, What, How?

In times of crisis, demand for government action in general and central planning in particular is sure to surge. The interwar era is a classic example. After the outbreak of the Great Depression in 1929, demand for economic planning—in contrast to capitalist market "anarchy"—was voiced in many countries. And not only voiced. The 1930s was an era of populism, nationalism, protectionism, government intervention and attempts to create planned economies. To some extent, the planning ideas were based on experiences from (not always successful) economic mobilization during World War I.

After World War II, the debate on economic planning resurged. This time, the impulse came not from an actual crisis, but from fear of a post-war depression like the one after World War I, and from (fairly successful) economic mobilization during the war. However, this thrust for planning pretty much stalled when the crisis refused to appear and when Keynesian crisis management overtook the scene.

After some "golden" decades, characterized by robust economic growth, crisis symptoms reappeared in the 1970s, this time in the shape of runaway oil prices and stagflation. Now the diagnosis of what was wrong went in the opposite direction: sclerosis due to heavy taxes and regulation. Keynesian policies gave way to monetarism and supply-side economics. With the downfall of the Soviet empire, ideas of economic planning seemed to belong to the past. Sweden at the same time experienced a largely home-made crisis, but since both state (expanding public expenditure) and market (a deregulated credit market) could be blamed, no distinct ideological overturn occurred.[1]

With the Great Recession of 2008, structural change due to globalization, waves of migration and impending climate change, the tide turned again. A new era of populism, nationalism, protectionist threats and demand for planning began. Soviet style planning was out of the picture, but planning advocates had a new "role model" in sight.

---

[1]A summary of these events, and the learning process they entailed, is given in L. Jonung, *Looking Ahead Through the Rear-View Mirror: Swedish Stabilisation Policy as a Learning Process 1970–1995* (Stockholm: Ministry of Finance, 2000).

How come Chinese "state capitalism" could achieve such high rates of growth, construct so much infrastructure and (plan to) tackle environmental challenges?

At all times, the notion of economic planning or planned economy has triggered ado. "The whole subject remains highly controversial, and ideologies of both left and right heavily influence both policies and theoretical formulations".[2] "The term 'planning' often stirs emotions".[3] What then is economic planning? A straightforward definition is "the allocation of resources by means other than markets". "For academic economists, including those involved in the debates of the 1930s, this definition is the usual one and uncontroversial".[4]

A recurring pattern during economic and other upheavals is demand for action coming from below (populism) and above (elitism). As Sheri Berman puts it, these two demands feed of another: "As should by now be painfully clear, technocracy and populism are mutually reinforcing; they feed of and strengthen one another".[5] They can be seen as "evil political twins".[6] At the end of the day, these two seemingly opposite currents tend to merge. With populism, the frustrated masses serve as a springboard for authoritarian leaders. With elitism, the ignorant masses are to be excluded from political decision-making in favour of enlightened technocrats.[7] In both cases, top-down economic policies with restrained democratic deliberation will result. A market economy may prevail, in some cases (like in today's United States) even get more leeway, but political democracy will be suppressed since it is associated with either too much talk and too little action (populism) or popular ignorance (elitism) and might obstruct unequivocal commands from

---

[2]A. Nove, "Planned Economy", in *The New Palgrave: Problems of the Planned Economy*, ed. J. Eatwell, M. Milgate, and P. Newman (London and Basingstoke: Macmillan, 1990), 197.

[3]T. Kowalik, "Central Planning", in *The New Palgrave: Problems of the Planned Economy*, ed. J. Eatwell, M. Milgate, and P. Newman (London and Basingstoke: Macmillan, 1990), 42.

[4]J. Tomlinson, "Planning: Debate and Policy in the 1940s", *Twentieth Century British History* 3(2) (1992): 154.

[5]S. Berman, "Populism Is a Problem. Elitist Technocrats Aren't the Solution", *Foreign Policy*, December 20, 2017.

[6]S. Berman, "Against the Technocrats", *Dissent* (Winter 2018).

[7]See, e.g., J. Brennan, *Against Democracy* (Princeton: Princeton University Press, 2016).

above. The major difference is that in the first case, people abdicate from their democratic rights voluntarily—they might, in the worst case, move into a state of "acclamatory democracy" (with a strong man ranting from a tribune surrounded by a hysterical crowd)—whereas in the second case, people will probably try to revolt. In the first case, the leader(s) will often be ignorant and in the second case, knowledgeable. In both cases, they will inevitably, as time goes by, be corrupt.

The ambition of this book is to survey the arguments for and against economic planning as they were put forward by leading Swedish economists in the 1930s and to put these arguments into a context of events and inspirational sources.[8] The choice of time period is motivated by the fact that this was the first extensive Swedish debate on economic planning—most arguments were repeated in the 1940s and by then, the Swedish debate was heavily influenced by arguments from abroad, particularly by Friedrich von Hayek's *The Road to Serfdom* (1944)[9]— and that it unfolded during and after a Great Depression; it thus seems relevant in comparison to our own time, in the aftermath of a Great Recession.[10] The choice of leading economists as key players is motivated by a desire to intercept stringent arguments and by the fact that I am myself an economic historian.

The Swedish debate on economic planning began in the mid-1920s, took off in 1930, culminated in 1934 and then gradually receded. This can be illustrated by a graph (Fig. 1.1) displaying the number of mentions of the word planned economy (in Swedish: *planhushållning*) in the database of digitized Swedish newspapers provided by the Swedish Royal Library.[11]

---

[8]Expositions of arguments for and against economic planning are given in E. Lipson, *A Planned Economy or Free Enterprise: The Lessons of History* (London: Adam & Charles Black, 1946), and, with some emphasis on regional and city planning, R. E. Klosterman, "Arguments for and Against Planning", *The Town Planning Review* 56(1) (1985).

[9]F. A. Hayek, *The Road to Serfdom* (London: Routledge, 1944). Hayek's book was immediately translated into Swedish.

[10]A renewed interest in economic planning has, in the Swedish context, been noted in M. Svensson, *Vad vi kan lära av planekonomin* (Stockholm: Timbro, 2017) and a pretty far-reaching parallel between the 1930s and our own times is drawn in B. Elmbrant, *Innan mörkret faller: Ska 30-talet hinna ifatt oss?* (Stockholm: Atlas, 2017).

[11]The figures are not fixed once and for all, since digitization is an ongoing effort, but the picture is telling enough.

Fig. 1.1 The word "planhushållning" in Swedish newspapers 1929–1939 (*Source* https://tidningar.kb.se [August 12, 2018])

The ambitions and limitations of the book can furthermore be stated as follows:

Firstly, this field of study requires considerable delimitations. One must focus upon certain features of central and long-term planning and—to make things simple—upon contexts where the terms economic planning or planned economy (*planhushållning*) are actually used. One cannot plunge into all kinds of policy debates on fiscal, monetary, social, agricultural, trade, crisis and unemployment policies, to name a few. Now, these delimitations are not always clear-cut. In particular, crisis/business cycle/unemployment policy is sometimes difficult to separate from economic planning, especially since Keynesian ideas first inspired and later somewhat eclipsed planning ambitions. However, one cannot, without deviating from the main theme, go into deep discussions of "Keynesianism" (countercyclical or full employment policies), which, just like the debate on economic planning, took place between older market liberal and younger state interventionist economists.[12]

Secondly, the Swedish debate must be put into a context of events and debates abroad. When glancing in different directions, one must draw a line between pure socialist/communist planning—where state

---

[12]For an overview of this discussion, see, e.g., B. Carlson, *The State as a Monster: Gustav Cassel and Eli Heckscher on the Role and Growth of the State* (Lanham: University Press of America, 1994), Chapter 12.

ownership of the means of production and central planning go hand in hand—and economic planning in market (or rather, mixed) economies. For this reason, I will try to stay away from discussions of socialism in general, which is tricky when planning represents one side of the socialist coin, and from the vast literature on Soviet style planning. This kind of planning, of course, to some extent, served as a source of inspiration for socialists in Western countries like Sweden, but not for Swedish economists.[13] The impetus in the Swedish debate on economic planning came mainly from Britain and the United States and, consequently, some introductory summaries of events in those countries will follow. Events in the Soviet Union (the five-year plans introduced in 1928 to build up heavy industry), in Italy (corporatism) and in Nazi Germany (the four-year plan introduced in 1936 to prepare for war) will only be touched upon when they appear in the Swedish debate.[14] They *did* appear quite often, but mainly as scarecrows.

To trace influences on Swedish economists from debates on economic planning in other countries is, however, a tricky business, simply because they seldom provided references. It is furthermore difficult to compare arguments (and the timing of them) in other countries with arguments launched in Sweden. In the former (international) case, we can just summarize some main points, whereas in the latter (Swedish) case, we are to follow the stream of arguments in detail. Our conclusions will thus have to focus on what played out on the Swedish scene.

---

[13]Classic texts on Soviet style central planning by economists like Herbert Levine, Alex Nove, Wassily Leontief, and Robert Campbell are collected in *Capitalism, Market Socialism, and Central Planning: Readings in Comparative Economic Systems*, ed. W. A. Leeman (Boston: Houghton Mifflin Company, 1963). A comprehensive exposition is given in E. H. Carr and R. W. Davies, *A History of Soviet Russia 9–14: Foundations of a Planned Economy, 1926–1929* (London: Macmillan, 1969–1978).

[14]For a comparison of Soviet and Nazi planning, see P. Temin, "Soviet and Nazi Economic Planning in the 1930s", *Economic History Review* 44(4) (1991): 574. Temin regards these two types of planning as very similar, focused on military mobilization and "prey to the vagaries of large and chaotic bureaucracies". The main differences were that in the Soviet Union private property was virtually non-existent, the initial level of industrialization was much lower and consumption much more suppressed.

Thirdly, it would be nice to be able to reach some firm conclusions about the effects of the Swedish economists' arguments upon politicians' arguing and decision-making. However, such an ambition would require a book of its own, which would be very difficult to write. As Alan Budd notes in his book *The Politics of Economic Planning*, "it is extremely difficult to determine the impact of economic knowledge on [political] decisions", partly because economists have diverging opinions and give different advice, partly because "politicians generally refer neither to economists, nor to economic theories when announcing decisions, so we can only dimly detect the implied theory and its author".[15] We have to settle for some general judgements about the impact of key players in the game.

Fourthly, to estimate the viability of Swedish arguments in a longer and broader perspective, they can tentatively be compared to arguments in the most famous book ever written on the issue of planned economies, Hayek's *The Road to Serfdom*, and to the arguments of one of Hayek's sharpest critics, E. F. M. Durbin.

As can be gathered from Fig. 1.1, much of the material in this study is collected from newspaper articles. Books and pamphlets are, of course, also used. The meetings in the Swedish Economic Society (*Nationalekonomiska Föreningen*), a forum for discussions among economists and people from business life, constitute another important source.

The book is organized as follows. A preliminary overview of the 1930s' debate on planned economy in Sweden is sketched, mainly based on Leif Lewin's "classic" dissertation from 1967. The main events and actors in the British, American and, to some extent, Continental debates on planning are presented. The Swedish main actors—the economists—are introduced. After all these preliminaries, the story of the Swedish economists in the debate on economic planning is told in a chronological manner. Finally, as always, the story is summarized and some conclusions are suggested.

---

[15]A. Budd, *The Politics of Economic Planning* (Manchester: Manchester University Press, 1978), 18.

Background

Political scientist Herbert Tingsten, in his seminal work on Swedish Social Democracy (first published in 1941), emphasized the influence from British liberalism and socialism in the 1920s through Ernst Wigforss, alongside Gunnar Myrdal "the most ingenious theoretician in the party".[16] At the beginning of the 1930s, Swedish Social Democrats could view the economic crisis as the final crisis of capitalism and unleash socialization or go for reforms within the frame of the existing system. The party congress of 1932 decided to pursue an active crisis policy without putting socialization on top of the agenda. The principle of socialization was replaced by the welfare ideology. The original Marxist ideology of the Swedish Social Democracy vaporized. Tingsten thus painted a picture of ideological disarmament and did not recall any battle over planning.[17]

Economist Karl-Gustav Landgren, in his dissertation on "the new economics" in Sweden (1960), followed impulses from the Liberal Party in Britain into the Swedish economic debate. These impulses emanated mainly from three sources: *Britain's Industrial Future* ("The Yellow Book") (1928), *We Can Conquer Unemployment* (1928) and John Maynard Keynes' and H. D. Henderson's *Can Lloyd George Do It?* (1929). Landgren's main point is that it was a politician, Ernst Wigforss (Minister of Finance 1925–1926 and 1932–1949), and not the economists, who first got the message and worked out a new theory and political programme: "It may be asserted that E. Wigforss was familiar with these ideas several years before Myrdal and Ohlin worked out the theory of an expansion program".[18] This initiative led Social Democrats to suggest a public works programme against unemployment at the 1930 *Riksdag* and to launch such a programme when they two years later rose to power. Among Swedish economists, Bertil Ohlin was the first to grasp

---

[16]H. Tingsten, *Den svenska socialdemokratins utveckling 2* (Stockholm: Bokförlaget Aldus/Bonniers, [1941] 1967), 362.

[17]A couple of years after Tingsten had published his analysis, he fought alongside Eli Heckscher against economic planning.

[18]K.-G. Landgren, *Den nya ekonomien' i Sverige: J. M. Keynes, E. Wigforss, B. Ohlin och utvecklingen 1927–1939* (Stockholm: Almqvist & Wiksell, 1960), 295.

the significance of the British (Keynesian) ideas. Landgren's dissertation led to a lively debate among economists and economic historians.[19] However, all participants in this debate were focused on "the new economics", on theories and policies designed to explain and combat unemployment, not on economic planning in a wider sense. It may be difficult, but nonetheless necessary, to draw a line between these issues in order not to get lost in the maze of writings on economists associated with the Stockholm school (*Stockholmsskolan*) and Keynesianism in Sweden.

Political scientist Leif Lewin's dissertation from 1967 is the "classic" exposition of the debate on economic planning in Sweden.[20] Lewin assigns most of his space to the debate of the 1940s but in his two first chapters recalls the debate on planning before and during the 1930s. According to Lewin, the front-line went between the "bourgeois" (non-socialist) camp, characterized by the liberal doctrine of harmony and freedom *from* state intervention, and the Social Democratic camp, characterized by Marxist fatalism and freedom *through* state intervention.[21] During the 1920s, the Social Democrats were caught between reformist ambitions in the short run and the idea of automatic progress towards socialism in the long run. New ideas, developed by Keynes and other Liberals in Britain, about the use of public works to increase demand and eliminate unemployment, helped the Swedish Social Democracy to get out of this trap. A decisive step was taken by Wigforss, when he at the Social Democratic party congress in 1932 explained that

---

[19]Wigforss himself claimed that the new crisis programme would have been launched even without inspiration from British Liberals. He pointed to socialist ideas in general and discussions within the British labour movement, from the *Minority Report to the Poor Law Commission* of 1909 to G. D. H. Cole's articles in *The New Statesman* in the 1920s. See E. Wigforss, "Den nya ekonomiska politiken", *Ekonomisk Tidskrift* 62(3) (1960).

[20]L. Lewin, *Planhushållningsdebatten* (Stockholm: Almqvist & Wiksell, 1967). The dissertation is in Swedish but there is a separate summary in English: L. Lewin, *The Debate on the Planned Economy in Sweden: Summary of the Dissertation "Planhushållningsdebatten"* (Uppsala, 1967). My summary, however, departs from the original dissertation in Swedish language. Later on, Lewin took up the theme once more as a chapter in a book on Swedish politics during 100 years, but only dealt with the 1940s debate. See L. Lewin, *Ideology and Strategy: A Century of Swedish Politics* (Cambridge: Cambridge University Press, 1988).

[21]In his memoirs, Ohlin was very critical of Lewin's lumping together of Conservatives and Liberals in a "bourgeois" camp. This is not surprising, given that Ohlin himself was a Liberal, non-socialist planning advocate. See B. Ohlin, *Ung man blir politiker* (Stockholm: Bonniers, 1972).

socialization and planning are two different things: "By socialization Wigforss meant nationalization; by economic planning 'a more general command of economic life' without any nationalization".[22] According to Lewin, this did not imply any breach in Social Democratic thought since there is a continuity between Marx' and Keynes' theories on underconsumption, unemployment and crises, but nevertheless there was a shift in perspective which released Social Democracy from its paralysis.[23]

The non-socialist actors figured that the crisis was a means to restore economic equilibrium, which had been upset by excessive wages and insufficient savings. The Social Democrats, however, now asserted that income created by public works would spread like ripples on water (multiplier effects) and boost consumption (demand) and thereby restore equilibrium. They entered the electoral campaign of 1932 with new-won self-esteem and a programme against unemployment. According to Lewin, this offensive had no equivalent anywhere else:

> It was something extraordinary also from an international perspective. No other political party in the world had a corresponding program of action against the world crisis. The conviction that they were right not only from a moral but also from an economic point of view is [...] a novelty in Social Democratic agitation. Intellectually inferior to the [market] liberal agitation and its harmony theory, Social Democratic propaganda had in the 1920 s been hampered by the fact that the non-socialists seemed to be able to "prove" that socialist economic policy was "impossible". Leading

---

[22]Lewin, *Planhushållningsdebatten*, 74.

[23]Tingsten objected that the Social Democrats had freed themselves from Marxist fatalism already at the end of WWI and he called the idea that they followed in Keynes' footsteps since they had followed in those of Marx arbitrary. See H. Tingsten, "Socialisering och planhushållning", *Tiden* 59(8) (1967). Lewin naturally defended his position in L. Lewin, "Ideologi och ekonomi", *Tiden* 59(10) (1967). A lengthy critique by Diane Sainsbury was countered by Lewin in a damning rejoinder. See D. Sainsbury, "A Critique of Leif Lewin's Planhushållningsdebatten", *Statsvetenskaplig Tidskrift* 71(2) (1968); and L. Lewin, "Kritisk traditionsförmedling: Ett genmäle", *Statsvetenskaplig Tidskrift* 72(1) (1969). We need not recount these arguments. We can just note that there is no doubt whatsoever about the fact that a lively debate on economic planning erupted in the early 1930s (see Fig. 1.1), just as claimed and told by Lewin.

Social Democrats had now figured out that this liberal economic theory was to a large extent wrong; many of its ideas had to make way for propositions which instead favored the socialist, state interventionist outlook.[24]

The parliamentary elections of 1932 resulted—after some logrolling with the Agrarian Party—in a Social Democratic government which launched a public works programme. The Social Democrats, as Lewin sees the matter, advanced firstly by measures to combat and avoid crises, and secondly by investigations focused on structural reforms and economic planning aimed at improved long-term efficiency of trade and industry regardless of economic fluctuations. Economic historian Kurt Wickman also argues that the short-term crisis policy of the 1930s contained the seeds of more long-term planning. The discussions in the committee of inquiry on unemployment in 1931–1935 and the way of financing the crisis policy—by balancing the national budget over the period of a complete business cycle—provided fertile ground for these seeds.[25]

The battle on economic planning erupted in earnest in 1934, when the Social Democrats announced more state action even though recovery was on its way. The economy was to "run at full speed" propelled by continued measures against unemployment and by structural reforms. A so-called Mammoth investigation was commissioned to deal with a number of economic and social issues. The Social Democratic ambitions were, according to Lewin, to avoid future economic crises and to increase economic efficiency through rationalization. The non-socialists questioned these ambitions, accused the Social Democrats of blind faith in the state and pointed to the lack of understanding of business issues among politicians and bureaucrats.

---

[24]Lewin, *Planhushållningsdebatten*, 95–96.

[25]K. Wickman, *Makroekonomisk planering—orsaker och utveckling* (Uppsala: Almqvist & Wiksell International, 1980).

When a reform pause was announced in 1938, the planning debate receded, and when the war broke out in 1939, the situation was radically different; an economy in preparedness for war is by definition a planned economy. The second battle on economic planning erupted at the end of World War II when Social Democrats announced their ambition to pursue economic planning even in time of peace.

According to Lewin's historiography, the planning debate of the 1930s can thus be dated to the years 1934–1938. It involves two opposite camps, Social Democrats and non-socialists, although Lewin certainly mentions other actors, particularly the Communists, who fought for revolution and Soviet style planning, and the Nazis, who fought for planning of a corporatist kind. He devotes some space to four economists: Gustav Cassel, Eli Heckscher, Gösta Bagge and Bertil Ohlin. Cassel, Heckscher and Bagge represent market liberalism within the non-socialist camp. Ohlin, with his concept of framework planning (*ramhushållning*), represents a social liberal intermediate position. Gunnar Myrdal is mentioned by Lewin for having in 1938 designed an agricultural policy acceptable to the Social Democrats in the longer run.[26]

In his review of the planning debate of the 1940s, Lewin somewhat plays down the importance of Hayek's *The Road to Serfdom* since similar ideas had been previously expressed in Sweden: "I just wish to recall Gustav Cassel's and Eli Heckscher's sharp defense of liberal freedom during the 1930s debate on economic planning".[27] Wickman draws the same conclusion: Heckscher and Cassel "anticipated Hayek's great work from 1944".[28]

Acknowledgements I am grateful to professors Lars Jonung and Mats Lundahl for their reviews of my manuscript. For any remaining errors, I have to thank myself.

---

[26]Myrdal went through the same kind of re-orientation as Wigforss. "The emphasis upon planning rather than nationalization came to play an increasingly important role in Gunnar Myrdal's vision of social democracy", writes T. Tilton, "Gunnar Myrdal and the Swedish Model", in *Gunnar Myrdal and His Works*, ed. G. Dostaler, D. Ethier, and L. Lepage (Montreal: Harvest House, 1992), 33.

[27]Lewin, *Planhushållningsdebatten*, 271.

[28]K. Wickman, "Eli Heckscher—pionjär utan efterföljare", in E. Heckscher, *Om staten, liberalismen och den ekonomiska politiken; texter i urval av Kurt Wickman* (Stockholm: Timbro, 2000), 41.

References

Berman, S. "Populism Is a Problem. Elitist Technocrats Aren't the Solution". *Foreign Policy*, December 20, 2017. http://foreignpolicy.com/2017/12/20/populism-is-a-problem-elitist-technocrats-arent-the-solution.

Berman, S. "Against the Technocrats". *Dissent* (Winter 2018). https://www.dissentmagazine.org/article/against-technocrats-liberal-democracy-history.

Brennan, J. *Against Democracy*. Princeton: Princeton University Press, 2016.

Budd, A. *The Politics of Economic Planning*. Manchester: Manchester University Press, 1978.

Carlson, B. *The State as a Monster: Gustav Cassel and Eli Heckscher on the Role and Growth of the State*. Lanham: University Press of America, 1994.

Carr, E. H., and R. W. Davies. *A History of Soviet Russia 9–14: Foundations of a Planned Economy, 1926–1929*. London: Macmillan, 1969–1978.

Elmbrant, B. *Innan mörkret faller: Ska 30-talet hinna ifatt oss?* Stockholm: Atlas, 2017.

Hayek, F. A. von. *The Road to Serfdom*. London: Routledge, 1944.

Jonung, L. *Looking Ahead Through the Rear-View Mirror: Swedish Stabilisation Policy as a Learning Process 1970–1995*. Stockholm: Ministry of Finance, 2000.

Klosterman, R. E. "Arguments for and Against Planning". *The Town Planning Review* 56(1) (1985): 5–20.

Kowalik, T. "Central Planning". In *The New Palgrave: Problems of the Planned Economy*, edited by J. Eatwell, M. Milgate, and P. Newman, 42–50. London and Basingstoke: Macmillan, 1990.

Landgren, K.-G. *Den nya ekonomien' i Sverige: J. M. Keynes, E. Wigforss, B. Ohlin och utvecklingen 1927–1939*. Stockholm: Almqvist & Wiksell, 1960.

Leeman, W. A. (ed.). *Capitalism, Market Socialism and Central Planning: Readings in Comparative Economic Systems*. Boston: Houghton Mifflin Company, 1963.

Lewin, L. "Ideologi och ekonomi". *Tiden* 59(10) (1967): 616–628.

Lewin, L. *Planhushållningsdebatten*. Stockholm: Almqvist & Wiksell, 1967.

Lewin, L. *The Debate on the Planned Economy in Sweden: Summary of the Dissertation "Planhushållningsdebatten".* Uppsala (No Publisher/Printer Stated), 1967.

Lewin, L. "Kritisk traditionsförmedling: Ett genmäle". *Statsvetenskaplig Tidskrift* 72(1) (1969): 21–42.

Lewin, L. *Ideology and Strategy: A Century of Swedish Politics.* Cambridge: Cambridge University Press, 1988.

Lipson, E. *A Planned Economy or Free Enterprise: The Lessons of History.* London: Adam & Charles Black, 1946.

Nove, A. "Planned Economy". In *The New Palgrave: Problems of the Planned Economy,* edited by J. Eatwell, M. Milgate, and P. Newman, 186–197. London and Basingstoke: Macmillan, 1990.

Ohlin, B. *Ung man blir politiker.* Stockholm: Bonniers, 1972.

Sainsbury, D. "A Critique of Leif Lewin's Planhushållningsdebatten". *Statsvetenskaplig Tidskrift* 71(2) (1968): 109–125.

Svensson, M. *Vad vi kan lära av planekonomin.* Stockholm: Timbro, 2017.

Temin, P. "Soviet and Nazi Economic Planning in the 1930s". *Economic History Review* 44(4) (1991): 573–593.

Tilton, T. "Gunnar Myrdal and the Swedish Model". In *Gunnar Myrdal and His Works,* edited by G. Dostaler, D. Ethier, and L. Lepage, 13–36. Montreal: Harvest House, 1992.

Tingsten, H. *Den svenska socialdemokratins utveckling 2.* Stockholm: Bokförlaget Aldus/Bonniers, [1941] 1967.

Tingsten, H. "Socialisering och planhushållning". *Tiden* 59(8) (1967): 463–476.

Tomlinson, J. "Planning: Debate and Policy in the 1940s". *Twentieth Century British History* 3(2) (1992): 154–174.

Wickman, K. *Makroekonomisk planering—orsaker och utveckling.* Uppsala: Almqvist & Wiksell International, 1980.

Wickman, K. "Eli Heckscher—pionjär utan efterföljare". In Heckscher, E., *Om staten, liberalismen och den ekonomiska politiken: Texter i urval av Kurt Wickman,* 11–52. Stockholm: Timbro, 2000.

Wigforss, E. "Den nya ekonomiska politiken". *Ekonomisk Tidskrift* 62(3) (1960): 185–194.

2

The International Context

Abstract The ambition in this chapter is to summarize debates and events in the 1920s and 1930s related to economic planning in Great Britain and the United States. The British case was complex; planning was "a word that was on everyone's lips and yet fractured by a multitude of interpretations and meanings". Planning ambitions in the US made an imprint around the world when Franklin Roosevelt in the spring of 1933 launched his New Deal. In both countries, the ideas of detailed planning was more or less eclipsed by John Maynard Keynes' "middle way" at the end of the 1930s. Furthermore, the so-called socialist calculation debate, which had been unfolding in German language on the European Continent in the 1920s, triggered by Ludwig von Mises, expanded into English language contributions in the 1930s. Friedrich von Hayek was probably the most outspoken economist against economic planning. He was challenged by E. F. M. Durbin, one of his colleagues at the London School of Economics.

Keywords Economic planning · Great Britain · United States · Socialist calculation debate

© The Author(s) 2018   **15**
B. Carlson, *Swedish Economists in the 1930s Debate
on Economic Planning*, Palgrave Studies in Economic History,
https://doi.org/10.1007/978-3-030-03700-0_2

Great Britain

If the Swedish debate on economic planning, as told by Leif Lewin, was fairly straightforward, with a Social Democratic and a "bourgeois" camp and a few extremists at the margins, the British case was all the more complicated. This case is important, since it was the main source of ideas injected into the Swedish debate, particularly by Ernst Wigforss and Bertil Ohlin. The complexity of the British case is made clear in Daniel Ritschel's 1997 book *The Politics of Planning: The Debate on Economic Planning in Britain in the 1930s*: Planning was "a word that was on everyone's lips and yet fractured by a multitude of interpretations and meanings"; "the planning debate was in many ways the most vivid example of the ideological fragmentation which characterized British politics in this turbulent decade".[1] In spite of this fragmentation, at least one basic idea was shared by planners from left to right:

> Its many proponents met in a shared rejection of *laissez-faire*, in the common belief that the market was not merely inefficient but also broken beyond repair. And in urging its replacement by a deliberately planned system. By the middle of the decade, the demand for a 'planned economy' of one type or another was heard in all parties and spanned practically the entire ideological spectrum of the day.[2]

The ideological differences were particularly evident in the perceptions of where the power ought to reside: with elected politicians, technocratic experts, a corporate state, organized workers or private industry. In other words: state socialism, technocracy, fascist corporatism, guild socialism or capitalist planning.

Ritschel treats the tug of war over the planning concept until the different movements converged towards John Maynard Keynes' "middle way" at the end of the decade. In the late 1920s, socialist maxims were frequent within the Labour Party. The Conservatives (Tories) turned against

---

[1]D. Ritschel, *The Politics of Planning: The Debate on Economic Planning in Britain in the 1930s* (Oxford: Clarendon Press, 1997), 330.

[2]Ibid., 4.

unfettered individualism and destructive competition and launched ideas on industrial rationalization to increase efficiency and decrease waste. Within the Liberal Party, Keynes worked on a "New Liberalism" aimed at a transition from capitalist anarchy to a regime of social justice and stability. The "Yellow Book" (1928) laid down guidelines for a mixed economy with organized private enterprise and state-owned or state-regulated companies. The planning idea had its breakthrough in 1930–1931:

> The term was invariably prefaced with adjectives like 'scientific', 'rational', and 'orderly', and juxtaposed with the 'chaos', 'anarchy', and 'irrationality' of the market economy. [—] The term served as a fashionable economic metaphor, an expressive antithesis to *laissez-faire*, strongly suggestive of the alternative of economic regulation to the disarray of the free-market economy, but undefined in any specific sense.[3]

Ritschel investigates six political movements pushing the planning idea in different directions.

Oswald Mosley launched his "New Party" in 1931. He attempted to merge elements from Keynesianism, socialism, Tory imperialism and Fordism, but had little patience with the democratic process. He claimed that his organic view of society was rooted in guild socialism, but he hardly followed socialist paths. "Yet for Mosley it came to serve as a rationale for the proto-fascist ideology of the Corporate State. [—] By mid-1931 Mosley had arrived at a position which was unmistakably fascist".[4] In the autumn of 1932, he launched the British Union of Fascists.

The Labour Party was in trouble. Ramsay McDonald's government resigned in August 1931. A national government was formed with McDonald as Prime Minister. The party suffered big losses in the October elections. Economic planning became a central element in its effort to revive its socialist ideology. The British Social Democrats, however, unlike their Swedish counterparts, insisted that planning and nationalization must go hand in hand. When the New Fabians stressed the importance of efficiency, they were met by the argument that

---

[3]Ibid., 48.
[4]Ibid., 90–91.

"[e]fficiency is not socialism".[5] The party could not close ranks. One faction aimed for the revisionist road, and another for the pure socialist road.

The Political and Economic Planning (PEP) Group, founded in 1931, was the first organization to argue for capitalist planning. It presented a national plan according to which industry would be organized into a series of councils supported by a "National Planning Commission", a body of economists and experts appointed by Parliament. Just like the Labour Party, this group was split into a moderate and a radical faction. One of the leading moderates, Sir Arthur Salter, advocated a "third way", a combination of planned structure and free enterprise.

The campaign for a Self-Government for Industry Bill in the mid-1930s represented "the climax of the idea of 'capitalist planning'".[6] In 1933, a business pressure group was set up with Harold Macmillan as chairman to lobby for such a bill. Macmillan belonged to the left wing of the Conservative Party and spoke of industrial self-government and "orderly capitalism" as a response to the threats of fascism and socialism. The bill was, however, dismissed by the party in 1935 because the conservative opinion was not considered ready for such a radical reform.

An attempt to frame a progressive centrist planning alternative was launched by the Next Five Years Group. The initiator was Clifford Allen, a Labour politician close to McDonald's loyalists. Allen argued for a reconstituted National government with economic planning on its programme. Three people dominated this group—Allen, Salter and Macmillan—and in 1935, *The Next Five Years: An Essay in Agreement* was published. The group met little sympathy from the Labour Party but saw a possible ally in David Lloyd George who in 1934 had launched his own New Deal.

The campaign for a Popular Front in 1936 was the last planning thrust in Britain, triggered by the need for progressive unity against threats posed by reactionary forces in other parts of Europe. Surprisingly, the initiative came from G. D. H. Cole, one of the principled socialists in the Labour Party. "His basic rationale was the

---

[5]Ibid., 116.
[6]Ibid., 183.

mounting tide of fascist violence in Europe, the growing threat of war, and the evident failure of the Labour party alone to mount an effective opposition to the government's disastrous course of 'vacillation' and 'half-sympathy with fascism'".[7]

Cole and Macmillan, representatives of socialist and capitalist planning, took on the task to forge a programme, but immediately recognized the significance of Keynes' *General Theory* when it was published in 1936.[8]

> Keynes's signal contribution to the Popular Front was thus to allow its two leading proponents to agree for the first time on a common economic agenda for the immediate future: full employment, the mixed economy, and state management of the aggregate level of economic activity. [—] Keynes […] did not provide the planners with either a final answer to the economic problem or a permanent resolution of their earlier conflict. But he supplied the grounds for a short-term tactical compromise […].[9]

Instead of forging a Popular Front, progressives to the left and right now rallied around Keynes' "middle way". Cole, however, retreated to his old plea for Soviet style planning, but the Labour Party moved in a reformist, Keynesian direction. On the progressive wing of the Conservative Party, this convergence was symbolized by Macmillan's book *The Middle Way* (1938). Finally, a quote from Alan Budd to underline Keynes' effect upon economic planning:

> The importance of Keynes in the debate on government intervention and in forming attitudes to planning cannot be overstated. He provided what most people believe is the main case for the state's role in managing the overall behavior of the economy. At the same time he destroyed the Labour Party's pre-war case for detailed planning.[10]

---

[7]Ibid., 282–283.

[8]J. M. Keynes, *The General Theory of Employment, Interest and Money* (London: Macmillan, 1936).

[9]Ritschel, *The Politics of Planning*, 303.

[10]A. Budd, *The Politics of Economic Planning* (Manchester: Manchester University Press, 1978), 32.

The United States

The US debate on economic planning made an imprint around the world when Franklin Roosevelt in the spring of 1933 launched his New Deal. William J. Barber's *Designs Within Disorder* (1996) offers one of the best surveys of planning discussions and efforts among the people whom he labels New Deal structural interventionists.

However, before plunging into New Deal events, it should be noted that Herbert Hoover as Secretary of Commerce 1921–1929 and President 1929–1933 was actually a pioneer within the field of economic planning. His stated ambition was to pursue "national planning", not by extending government powers but by supplying information to economic actors, not least business managers, through statistical publications, expert investigations and conferences.[11] In this way, Hoover experimented with "indicative planning" decades before this variety of planning came into fashion.

During the 1932 presidential campaign, two economists in Roosevelt's "Brain Trust" played a pivotal role: Adolf A. Berle and Rexford Guy Tugwell, both professors at Columbia University. Berle was of the opinion that the concentration within US industry, with gradually fewer corporate directors in control of the economy, indicated that the American and Russians systems would eventually converge, a development he approved of. Tugwell "rejected the doctrines of laissez-faire as unrealistic, wasteful and socially immoral".[12] He departed from the same kind of thought as Thorstein Veblen, according to which engineers and not businessmen ought to control the economy. Barber quotes the following from a speech by Tugwell before the American Economic Association in 1931: "Planning is by definition the opposite to conflict; its meaning is aligned to co-ordination, to rationality, to

---

[11]See W. J. Barber, *From New Era to New Deal: Herbert Hoover, the Economists, and American Economic Policy, 1921–1933* (Cambridge: Cambridge University Press, 1988); E. W. Hawley, "Herbert Hoover, the Commerce Secretariat, and the Vision of an 'Associative State', 1921–1928", *Journal of American History* 61(1) (1974); and E. W. Hawley (ed.), *Herbert Hoover as Secretary of Commerce: Studies in New Era Thought and Practice* (Iowa City: University of Iowa Press, 1981).

[12]W. J. Barber, *Designs Within Disorder: Franklin D. Roosevelt, the Economists, and the Shaping of American Economic Policy, 1933–1945* (Cambridge: Cambridge University Press, 1996), 6.

publicly defined and expertly approached aims; but not to private money-making ventures; and not to the guidance of a hidden hand ...".[13] As a first step, Tugwell proposed that industrial associations set up their own planning boards to regulate competition and that these boards be subject to oversight by a central body.

Ideas similar to Tugwell's were launched by some industrialists, particularly Gerard Swope, President of General Electric. According to the Swope Plan, trade associations should coordinate supply and demand with the purpose of stabilizing prices and wages. Both Tugwell and Swope thus wished to ignore the US antitrust laws. When Swope revealed his plan in 1931, president Hoover branded it as the most gigantic proposal of monopoly ever made in American history.

During his early days in power, Roosevelt signed two major laws, aimed at agriculture and industry, respectively, Agricultural Adjustment Act (AAA) and National Industrial Recovery Act (NIRA), the latter with the ambitious purpose "to promote cooperative action, eliminate unfair practices, increase purchasing power, expand production, reduce unemployment, and conserve natural resources" by dint of industrial "codes of fair competition".[14] The administrator of the National Recovery Administration (NRA), General Hugh Johnson, was a champion of industrial self-government, unlike Tugwell who was in favour of government control. The AAA, as is well known, aimed at cutting supply in order to raise prices, with startling actions such as the slaughter of six million pigs. In July 1933, Roosevelt, in one of his famous Fireside Chats, told the nation that NIRA aimed at planning for a "logical whole". However, the initial New Deal enthusiasm soon waned:

> When the National Industrial Recovery Act was being designed in the spring of 1933, the enthusiasts for "concentration and control" – as opposed to "competition and conflict" – were riding the crest of the wave.

---

[13]Ibid., 7. Wolfgang Schivelbusch highlights similarities between the regimes of Roosevelt, Mussolini and Hitler and quotes Tugwell stating in his diary that fascism is the "most efficiently operating piece of social machinery I've ever seen. It makes me envious". See W. Schivelbusch, *Three New Deals: Reflections on Roosevelt's America, Mussolini's Italy, and Hitler's Germany, 1933–1939* (New York: Picador, 2006), 32.

[14]Quoted from Barber, *Designs Within Disorder*, 29.

A new industrial order appeared to be within reach. Tugwell and those like-minded saw this legislation as a sea change in the functioning of the American economy. [...] By early 1934, much of this original enthusiasm had been spent. Results clearly did not measure up to expectations. [...] Codes that encouraged firms to limit production and to postpone investment [...] offered no formula for a return to prosperity. In the press, NRA was being pilloried as standing for "No Recovery Allowed", "National Retardation Association" or "National Run Around."[15]

The NRA came under crossfire from consumer and small business interests and from other public agencies. General Johnson fired back by telling Roosevelt that the NRA had to be reorganized as "a new form of government – an economic government superimposed upon a political government".[16] Here, one could literally talk of a general plan! Another economist influenced by Veblen, Gardiner C. Means,[17] was called upon to redesign industrial policy. He argued that the NRA and AAA were both responses to the failures of unregulated markets and that the policies of these agencies and the whole administration had to be coordinated in order to avoid contradiction and confusion. Such a policy should aim at "the smooth functioning of the economic machine, the full use of human and material resources, and a balance of interests among individuals and groups", mainly business, labour and consumers.[18]

In early 1935, yet another economist and institutionalist, John Maurice Clark, was brought in to untangle the NRA. He lauded much of what had been done and encouraged further experimentation. However, in May 1935, the Supreme Court struck down the NIRA, declaring its code-making to be an unconstitutional delegation of legislative power, and that "comprehensive planning for the industrial sector was dead".[19]

---

[15]Ibid., 53.

[16]Ibid., 59.

[17]Adolf Berle and Gardiner Means had co-authored the famous book *The Modern Corporation and Private Property* in 1932; the basic message was that ownership and management had been divorced in the modern corporation.

[18]Means, quoted in Barber, *Designs Within Disorder*, 62.

[19]Ibid., 67.

"Economists in the mainstream of orthodoxy rejoiced at the decision by the Supreme Court. Even among those sympathetic to experimentation, there was a widespread recognition that NRA had been a flawed instrument".[20]

A critical retrospect view of the NRA, displaying its complexity, can be found in Amity Shales' *Forgotten Man* (2007):

> The NRA was the consummation of a thousand articles and a thousand trends. It was the ideas of Moley, the trade unions, Stuart Chase, Tugwell, Stalin, Insull, Teddy Roosevelt, Henry Ford, and Mussolini's Italian model all rolled into one. The law worked on the assumption that bigger was better and that industry, labor, and government must work together, as in Italy, or risk staying in depression.[21]

A Supreme Court decision in January 1936 forced the AAA planners to find new ways to curtail agricultural production. They started subsidizing reallocation of acreage from "soil-depleting" to "soil-conserving" crops. The next setback for the New Dealers came with the 1937 recession. This event made economists, who had previously been sceptical towards Keynes' prescriptions, change their minds. The most renowned among these are Alvin Hansen and Lauchlin Currie. Roosevelt was also prepared to abandon his traditional fiscal prudence and called for a 3 billion dollar spending and lending programme. "Roosevelt's decision to embark unapologetically on a 'spend-lend' programme in April 1938 appeared to signal that the administration had come to terms with an Americanized version of Keynesian aggregate demand management".[22]

---

[20]Ibid., 68.

[21]A. Shales, *Forgotten Man: A New History of the Great Depression* (New York: HarperCollins, 1997), 151. Raymond Moley was professor of law at Columbia University. He recruited colleagues at Columbia to Roosevelt's original "Brain Trust", wrote speeches for Roosevelt and coined the term "the forgotten man". Stuart Chase was a member of the Veblenite technocracy movement and a Soviet Union admirer. In 1932, he wrote a book titled *A New Deal*. Samuel Insull was an entrepreneur within the electrical utilities industry.

[22]Barber, *Designs Within Disorder*, 116.

Mises, Hayek and Durbin

The so-called socialist calculation debate had been unfolding in German language on the European Continent in the 1920s; it expanded into English language contributions in the 1930s. This debate had been triggered by Ludwig von Mises' claim in his article on "Die Wirtschaftsrechnung im sozialistischen Gemeinwesen" and his following book *Die Gemeinwirtschaft* that a socialist economy in the absence of market-based prices would not be able to function in a rational way.[23] "Where there is no free market, there is no pricing mechanism; without a pricing mechanism, there is no economic calculation". Consequently: "There is only groping in the dark. Socialism is the abolition of rational economy".[24]

That Mises was somewhat known in Sweden at the time is demonstrated by the translation of his book *Liberalismus* into Swedish.[25] In it, he discussed a third way between capitalism and socialism where government interventions in the market mechanism (price formation) by its own dynamics must lead to complete government control of production and distribution:

> If government decides, what is to be produced, how it is to be produced, at what price and to whom it is to be sold, then nothing remains of private property but the name. All property is in reality nationalized, since the driving force for economic activity is no longer the quest for profit by entrepreneurs and property owners, but the compulsion to fulfill a duty, to obey a given command.[26]

---

[23]L. von Mises, *Gemeinwirtschaft: Untersuchungen über den Sozialismus* (Jena: Verlag von Gustav Fischer, 1922).

[24]L. von Mises, "Economic Calculation in the Socialist Commonwealth", in *Collectivist Economic Planning: Critical Studies on the Possibilities of Socialism*, ed. F. A. Hayek (Clifton: Augustus M. Kelley Publishers, [1935] 1975), 110–111. Originally in German in 1920.

[25]L. von Mises, *Kapitalism och socialism i de liberala idéernas belysning* (Stockholm: P. A. Norstedt & Söners Förlag, 1930). In the Royal Library digital newspaper database, Mises book is mentioned a few times in the 1930s, mainly in advertisements for book sales. Mises himself is only mentioned once in passing.

[26]Mises, *Kapitalism*, 66.

Mises set forth only two options: Refrain from interventions in the market mechanism or transfer all management of production and distribution to public authorities. "Either capitalism or socialism. There is no middle way".[27]

Hayek was already in the 1930s (and would be even more so in the 1940s) probably the most outspoken economist against economic planning.[28] In 1931, he was recruited by Lionel Robbins from Vienna to the London School of Economics (LSE). A couple of years later, he edited a book titled *Collectivist Economic Planning* in which he himself wrote two chapters, a book which has been labelled "the opening salvo in the English-language socialist calculation debate".[29]

In the introductory chapter, Hayek noted that "[t]he increasing preoccupation of the modern world with problems of an engineering character tends to blind people to the totally different character of the economic problem".[30] When the engineer decides on the best way to produce a commodity, his decision is economic only when he uses market prices as the basis for his calculation.[31] However, "the fact that in the present order of things such economic problems are not solved by the conscious decision of anybody has the effect that most people are not conscious of their existence". It was not necessary for the working of this system, that people should understand it. "But people are not likely to let it work if they do not understand it".[32]

---

[27]Ibid., 81. When Mises in 1945 delivered an address before the American Academy of Political and Social Sciences, he repeated this conclusion: "There is no middle way". See L. von Mises, "Planning for Freedom", in *Economic Planning*, ed. L. von Mises and R. F. Tucker (New York: Dynamic America, 1945), 12.

[28]In the Royal Library digital newspaper database, Hayek is only mentioned once in passing in the 1930s.

[29]B. Caldwell, *Hayek's Challenge: An Intellectual Biography of F. A. Hayek* (Chicago and London: The University of Chicago Press, 2005), 199.

[30]F. A. Hayek, "The Nature and History of the Problem", in *Collectivist Economic Planning: Critical Studies on the Possibilities of Socialism*, ed. F. A. Hayek (Clifton: Augustus M. Kelley Publishers, [1935] 1975), 4.

[31]Hayek thus had a completely opposite view compared to Veblen, whom he, however, did not mention.

[32]Hayek, "The Nature", 7–8.

Hayek argued that the German historical school in economics had caused a decay of economic insight and that it was no accident that Marxism had been most readily accepted in Germany. He went on to say that the problem of socialism as a method was "that one central authority has to solve the economic problem of distributing a limited amount of resources between a practically infinite number of competing purposes".[33] He noted that the Social Democratic interpretation of Marxism implied a questionable combination of collective ownership and central direction of all material resources of production with continued freedom of choice in consumption and occupation. He envisioned that planning efforts in a capitalist society would lead to total planning:

> In fact, however, if by planning is meant the actual direction of productive activity by authoritative prescription, either of the quantities to be produced, the methods of production to be used, or the prices to be fixed, it can be easily shown, not that such a thing is impossible, but that any isolated measure of this sort will cause reactions which will defeat its own end, and that any attempt to act consistently will necessitate further and further measures of control until all economic activity is brought under one central authority.[34]

To say that partial planning was irrational did, however, not mean that the only rational form of capitalism was "that of complete *laissez faire* in the old sense". "There is no reason to assume that the historically given legal institutions are necessarily the most 'natural' in any sense".[35] But there was a big difference between a legal framework devised to provide the necessary incentives to private initiatives to bring about adaptions required by change, and a system where such adaptions were brought about by central direction. The mixture of the 1930s was hopeless: "We are certainly as far from capitalism in its pure form as we are from any system of central planning. The world of to-day is just interventionist chaos".[36]

---

[33]Ibid., 16–17.
[34]Ibid., 21.
[35]Ibid., 22.
[36]Ibid., 23–24.

In the closing chapter, Hayek underscored that the calculation problem could hardly be solved in a mathematical way since it would require enormous amounts of information: "It is probably evident that the mere assembly of these data is a task beyond human capacity".[37] The magnitude of the mathematical operation depended upon the number of unknowns, equal to the number of commodities to be produced. In an advanced society, these could be counted in the hundreds of thousands.

> This means that, at each successive moment, every one of the decisions would have to be based on the solution of an equal number of simultaneous differential equations, a task which, with any of the means known at present, could not be carried out in a lifetime. And yet these decisions would not only have to be made continuously, but they would also have to be conveyed continuously to those who had to execute them.[38]

Hayek consequently concluded that "practically all, who have really tried to think through the problem of central planning, have despaired of the possibilities of solving it in a world in which every passing whim of the consumer is likely to upset completely the carefully worked out plan".[39] Free choice of consumption and probably also occupation were incompatible with central planning. Even if these choices were eliminated, there were hundreds of other constant changes which would upset the plan, changes in weather, population size and people's health, breakdowns of machinery, discovery or exhaustion of mineral deposits, etc. Hayek, however, sarcastically admitted that a planned system could score in one respect: "A centrally planned system, although it would not avoid making even more serious mistakes of the sort which lead to crises under capitalism, would at least have the advantage that it would be possible to share the loss equally between all its members".[40]

---

[37]F. A. Hayek, "The Present State of the Debate", in *Collectivist Economic Planning: Critical Studies on the Possibilities of Socialism*, ed. F. A. Hayek (Clifton: Augustus M. Kelley Publishers, [1935] 1975), 211.

[38]Ibid., 212.

[39]Ibid., 214.

[40]Ibid., 139. In Sweden, a famous dictum by Wigforss, that poverty is more easily accepted if shared equally by all, was often the subject of sarcastic comments.

When the Polish economist Oskar Lange claimed that trial and error could work better in a socialist economy than in a competitive market since a central planning authority has much wider knowledge of what is going on in the economy than any private entrepreneur can ever have, Hayek responded by saying that Lange was preoccupied with problems of the theory of static equilibrium. In the real world, constant change is the rule. There is thus no one-time adjustment of prices towards some final equilibrium but a never-ending process. Bruce Caldwell writes that "Hayek never rejected equilibrium theory; he always insisted it was good for *certain* uses" but "he felt that it led people to draw the wrong conclusions about the nature of the market process".[41]

Britain in the 1930s was, as we have seen, a playground for planning advocates of different political colours. Among intellectuals, Sidney and Beatrice Webb advocated Soviet style planning and sociologist Karl Mannheim preached the abandonment of liberal democracy and acceptance of a planning authority with unlimited powers: "if one wants things done, the responsible director of affairs must be freed from the fetters of democratic procedure".[42] Hayek complained that for every hundred scientists attacking competition and capitalism, there was only one resisting the planners. Nonetheless, he had allies, like Lionel Robbins at LSE, Walter Lippman in the United States and in Germany Wilhelm Roepke (after 1933 in Turkey and Switzerland) and Michael Polanyi (after 1933 in Britain).

In 1936, E. F. M. Durbin, an economist at LSE, challenged the central argument in *Collectivist Economic Planning*. He agreed with Hayek "that the solution of a system of simultaneous equations by the Central Authority is not a practicable procedure", but attempted to demonstrate an alternative system, "the theoretical possibility of a pricing system in a Planned Economy", a demonstration which is hardly possible to summarize in a few sentences.[43] The year before, Durbin had exclaimed that "we

---

[41]Caldwell, *Hayek's Challenge*, 226.

[42]Mannheim quoted in Caldwell, ibid., 240.

[43]E. F. M. Durbin, *Problems of Economic Planning* (London: Routledge & Kegan Paul, 1949), 140, 155. This book contains eleven previously published papers/articles. Particularly interesting in the present context are "The Importance of Planning" from 1935 and "Economic Calculus in a Planned Economy" from 1936.

are all *Planners* now" and mobilized a battery of arguments for planning.[44] He defined planning as "the extension of the size of the unit of management and the consequent enlargement of the field surveyed when any economic decision is taken" and claimed that planning "does not in the least imply the existence of a Plan [...]. Planning does not, and should not, imply any dogmatism about the future".[45] He refuted the argument that planning "will lead to chaos because it lacks the automatic guide of pricing" by pointing to the Russian five-year plan, "based fundamentally upon prices" and stating that "there is no formal or logical contradiction between planning and pricing".[46] He advanced mainly two arguments for planning: increased efficiency and increased stability. Efficiency would be increased through better overview ("an economy with open eyes"):

A central authority [...] can see things no individual producer can ever see and give weight to considerations that cannot play any part in the calculation of men engaged in competition with one another. The general officers on the hill must be able to see more than the ensign in the line of battle.[47]

Increased foresight in time would result in a better relation between finance and production and thus in greater economic stability. Durbin readily admitted that these gains could not be achieved unless "there is a willingness on the part of the organized labour to adjust itself to the new conditions of national control". All workers must "be prepared to allow their own interests to be subordinated to the interests of the workers as a whole", i.e. to the planning authority. And not only workers: "the interests of all should be served by a continuous process of concession on the part of particular groups". Durbin finally emphasized the importance of the spirit behind planning: "The efficiency of Planning depends in the last resort upon the breadth and consistency of the Socialist faith which animates us".[48]

---

[44]Ibid., 41.
[45]Ibid., 43–44.
[46]Ibid., 46–48.
[47]Ibid., 51.
[48]Ibid., 56–57.

References

Barber, W. J. *From New Era to New Deal: Herbert Hoover, the Economists, and American Economic Policy, 1921–1933*. Cambridge: Cambridge University Press, 1988.

Barber, W. J. *Designs Within Disorder: Franklin D. Roosevelt, the Economists, and the Shaping of American Economic Policy, 1933–1945*. Cambridge: Cambridge University Press, 1996.

Budd, A. *The Politics of Economic Planning*. Manchester: Manchester University Press, 1978.

Caldwell, B. *Hayek's Challenge: An Intellectual Biography of F.A. Hayek*. Chicago and London: The University of Chicago Press, 2005.

Durbin, E. F. M. *Problems of Economic Planning*. London: Routledge & Kegan Paul, 1949.

Hawley, E. W. "Herbert Hoover, the Commerce Secretariat, and the Vision of an 'Associative State', 1921–1928". *Journal of American History* 61(1) (1974): 116–140.

Hawley, E. W. (ed.). *Herbert Hoover as Secretary of Commerce: Studies in New Era Thought and Practice*. Iowa City: University of Iowa Press, 1981.

Hayek, F. A. von. "The Nature and History of the Problem". In *Collectivist Economic Planning: Critical Studies on the Possibilities of Socialism*, edited by F. A. Hayek, 1–40. Clifton: Augustus M. Kelley Publishers, [1935] 1975.

Hayek, F. A. von. "The Present State of the Debate". In *Collectivist Economic Planning: Critical Studies on the Possibilities of Socialism*, edited by F. A. Hayek, 201–243. Clifton: Augustus M. Kelley Publishers, [1935] 1975.

Keynes, J. M. *The General Theory of Employment, Interest and Money*. London: Macmillan, 1936.

Mises, L. von. *Gemeinwirtschaft: Untersuchungen über den Sozialismus*. Jena: Verlag von Gustav Fischer, 1922.

Mises, L. von. *Kapitalism och socialism i de liberala idéernas belysning*. Stockholm: P. A. Norstedt & Söners Förlag, 1930.

Mises, L. von. "Economic Calculation in the Socialist Commonwealth". In *Collectivist Economic Planning: Critical Studies on the Possibilities of Socialism*, edited by F. A. Hayek, 87–130. Clifton: Augustus M. Kelley Publishers, [1935] 1975.

Mises, L. von. "Planning for Freedom". In *Economic Planning*, edited by L. von Mises and R. F. Tucker, 1–14. New York: Dynamic America, 1945.

Ritschel, D. *The Politics of Planning: The Debate on Economic Planning in Britain in the 1930s*. Oxford: Clarendon Press, 1997.

Schivelbusch, W. *Three New Deals: Reflections on Roosevelt's America, Mussolini's Italy, and Hitler's Germany, 1933–1939*. New York: Picador, 2006.

Shales, A. *Forgotten Man: A New History of the Great Depression*. New York: HarperCollins, 1997.

3

The Swedish Economists

Abstract Five Swedish economists were at the heart of the Swedish debate on economic planning: Gustav Cassel, Eli Heckscher and Gösta Bagge represented an older generation of classical/market liberals opposed to planning, Bertil Ohlin and Gunnar Myrdal a younger generation of social liberals or socialists advocating planning. These five fought over economic planning from the late 1920s to the late 1930s. Cassel, Heckscher and Ohlin wrote in daily newspaper on a regular basis, Bagge and Myrdal were more directly involved in policy-making. A few other economists occasionally intervened in the debate: David Davidson, Sven Brisman, Karin Kock, Gustaf and Johan Åkerman. Ernst Wigforss, leading Social Democrat and the man who "divorced" planning from socialization, will also play a role in our story. He was not an economist by profession but anyway at the forefront of economic policy debates.

Keywords Swedish economists · Gustav Cassel · Eli Heckscher · Gösta Bagge · Gunnar Myrdal · Bertil Ohlin

© The Author(s) 2018
B. Carlson, *Swedish Economists in the 1930s Debate
on Economic Planning*, Palgrave Studies in Economic History,
https://doi.org/10.1007/978-3-030-03700-0_3

Five Swedish economists were at the heart of the Swedish debate on economic planning: Gustav Cassel, Eli Heckscher and Gösta Bagge belong to an older generation of classical/market liberals opposed to planning. Bertil Ohlin and Gunnar Myrdal belong to a younger generation of social liberals or socialists advocating planning. These five fought over economic planning from the late 1920s to the late 1930s.[1] Our story will to a large extent revolve around the "big five".[2]

- Gustav Cassel (1866–1945) was for a while after WWI the world's most famous economist, even more exposed in the international arena than Keynes.[3] He emerged as an economist around the turn of the century 1900, was professor of economics and finance at Stockholm University 1904–1934 and an influential voice in domestic debates on economic and social policy issues. Before WWI, he was a fairly radical liberal; in a book on social policy, he specified the roles which ought to be played by government, employers and trade unions.[4] His main theoretical contribution, *Theoretische Sozialökonomie*, appeared in 1918.[5] After the war, he turned into a conservative market liberal, a relentless critic of socialism, economic planning, public works, welfare and the like. During the 1920s, his star was in zenith as he participated in international conferences devoted to economic and particularly monetary matters in the aftermath of the war. In the 1930s, his star began to lose some of its lustre. He attempted to consolidate his reputation through a massive, two-volume memoir titled (if translated into English) "In the

---

[1]An overview of Swedish economists in the public debate is given in B. Carlson and L. Jonung, "Knut Wicksell, Gustav Cassel, Eli Heckscher, Bertil Ohlin and Gunnar Myrdal on the Role of the Economist in Public Debate", *Econ Journal Watch* 3(3) (2006).

[2]Portraits of these five and many other Swedish economists are available (in Swedish language) in C. Jonung and A.-C. Ståhlberg (eds.), *Svenska nationalekonomer under 400 år* (Stockholm: Dialogos, 2014).

[3]B. Carlson, "Who Was Most World-Famous—Cassel or Keynes? *The Economist* as Yardstick", *Journal of the History of Economic Thought* 31(4) (2009).

[4]G. Cassel, *Socialpolitik* (Stockholm: Hugo Gebers Förlag, 1902).

[5]G. Cassel, *Theoretische Sozialökonomie* (Leipzig: C.F. Winter, 1918); *The Theory of Social Economy* (London: T. Fisher Unwin, 1923).

Service of Reason".[6] It may thus seem as if Cassel over time shifted his weight from left to right in a drastic way. However, there was continuity in his posture. He always stressed the importance of economic growth. In his younger days, he thought that the working class was in a precarious situation; in his older days, he feared that capital formation was being compromised. Both these factors of production must be safeguarded if maximum economic efficiency was to be achieved.[7]

- Eli Heckscher (1879–1952) started out as historian and as a political social conservative; he called for a strong state elevated above all special interests. He was trained as an economist under David Davidson in Uppsala and Cassel in Stockholm and was particularly inspired by Alfred Marshall and Knut Wicksell. Heckscher was professor of economics and statistics at the Stockholm School of Economics (*Handelshögskolan*) from 1909. Like Cassel, he changed his ideological stance during (and even before) WWI,[8] published a programmatic book on old and new economic liberalism[9] and for the rest of his life fought against state interventionism. He repeatedly stressed that the ultimate purpose of economic activity is consumption. He was more of a principled liberal than Cassel and the two got into a dispute over tariffs in the 1920s. Heckscher was a demanding workaholic and had a tendency to get into conflict with colleagues.[10]

---

[6]G. Cassel, *I förnuftets tjänst*, Vols. 1–2 (Stockholm: Natur och Kultur, 1940–1941).

[7]Some English-language sources on Cassel: A. Montgomery, "Gustav Cassel, 1866–1945", *Economic Journal* 57(228) (1947); E. Lundberg, "The Influence of Gustav Cassel on Economic Doctrine and Policy", *Skandinaviska Banken Quarterly Review* 48(1) (1967); H. Brems, "Gustav Cassel Revisited", *History of Political Economy* 21(2) (1989); L. Magnusson, "Gustav Cassel, Popularizer and Enigmatic Walrasian", in *The History of Swedish Economic Thought*, ed. B. Sandelin (London and New York: Routledge, 1991); L. Pålsson-Syll, "Cassel and Revealed Preference Theory", *History of Political Economy* 25(3) (1993); P. Samuelson, "Gustav Cassel's Scientific Innovations: Claims and Realities", *History of Political Economy* 25(3) (1993); and B. Carlson, *The State as a Monster: Gustav Cassel and Eli Heckscher on the Role and Growth of the State* (Lanham: University Press of America, 1994).

[8]B. Carlson, "Eli Heckscher's Ideological Migration Toward Market Liberalism", *Econ Journal Watch* 13(1) (2016).

[9]E. Heckscher, *Gammal och ny ekonomisk liberalism* (Stockholm: P. A. Norstedt & Söner, 1921).

[10]See Y. Hasselberg, *Industrisamhällets förkunnare: Eli Heckscher, Arthur Montgomery, Bertil Boëthius och svensk ekonomisk historia 1920–1950* (Hedemora/Möklinta: Gidlunds Förlag, 2007); M. Lundahl, *Seven Figures in the History of Swedish Economic Thought: Knut Wicksell, Eli*

This foiled his ambition to become president of the Stockholm School of Economics. He was compensated with a personal research professorship in economic history (1929–1945) and produced extensive works on mercantilism and Sweden's economic history.[11] Among economists, his international reputation stems to a large extent from a 1919 article,[12] which was later elaborated by Ohlin into the so-called Heckscher-Ohlin theorem.[13]

- Gösta Bagge (1882–1951) is today a rather forgotten name. However, he was once an influential economist and politician, often labelled entrepreneur within in these areas.[14] As a young man, he studied in 1904–1905 at Johns Hopkins University and became interested in trade union and labour market issues,[15] which led to a momentous doctoral dissertation on the regulation of wages through collective bargaining.[16] In 1921, Bagge became professor of economics and social policy at Stockholm University and founded his

---

Heckscher, Bertil Ohlin, Torsten Gårdlund, Sven Rydenfelt, Staffan Burenstam Linder and Jamie Behar (Houndmills, Basingstoke, Hampshire: Palgrave Macmillan, 2015).

[11]E. Heckscher, Mercantilism I-II (London: Allen & Unwin, 1935); E. Heckscher, Sveriges ekonomiska historia från Gustav Vasa I-II (Stockholm: Albert Bonniers Förlag, 1935–1936).

[12]E. Heckscher, "Utrikeshandelns verkan på inkomstfördelningen: Några teoretiska grundlinjer", Nationalekonomiska studier tillägnade professor David Davidson, Ekonomisk Tidskrift 21(2) (1919). This article was eventually published in English: E. Heckscher, "The Effect of Foreign Trade on the Distribution of Income", in Heckscher-Ohlin Trade Theory, ed. H. Flam and J. Flanders (Cambridge, MA and London: MIT Press, 1991).

[13]Some English-language sources on Heckscher: C. G. Uhr, "Eli F. Heckscher, 1879–1952, and His Treatise on Mercantilism Revisited", Economy and History 23(1) (1980); R. G. H. Henriksson, "Eli F. Heckscher: The Economic Historian as Economist", in The History of Swedish Economic Thought, ed. B. Sandelin (London and New York: Routledge, 1991); Carlson, The State as a Monster; R. Findlay et al. (eds.), Eli Heckscher, International Trade and Economic History (Cambridge, MA and London: MIT Press, 2006); Lundahl, Seven Figures in the History of Swedish Economic Thought. Heckscher's most important writings on economic planning are reprinted in E. Heckscher, Om staten, liberalismen och den ekonomiska politiken: Texter i urval av Kurt Wickman (Stockholm: Timbro, 2000).

[14]E. Wadensjö, "Gösta Bagge: An Entrepreneur in Swedish Economics", in Swedish Economic Thought: Explorations and Advances, ed. L. Jonung (London and New York: Routledge, 1993).

[15]B. Carlson, "Gösta Bagge's American Lessons", Scandinavian Economic History Review 39(2) (1991).

[16]G. Bagge, Arbetslönens reglering genom sammanslutningar (Stockholm: AB Nordiska Bokhandeln, 1917).

own Social Institute. He launched a major research project, funded by grants from the Rockefeller Foundation, on national income, wages and cost of living, in which several of the young economists who later formed the Stockholm school (*Stockholmsskolan*) were involved.[17] He was active as politician in the City of Stockholm and as a key member of the Committee on Unemployment appointed in 1927.[18] Thereafter, his political ambitions took over. He became member of the *Riksdag* in 1932, leader of the Conservative Party in 1935 and Minister of Education in the WWII government of national unity.[19] He will more or less fade away from our story in 1935 since he was from that time a full-time politician and not an economist. After all, a party leader cannot express his views freely but must to some degree follow "the party line".

● Gunnar Myrdal (1898–1987) started out as a conservative inspired by political scientist Rudolf Kjellén, a nationalist and anti-liberal state activist who launched the concept of "People's Home" before WWI. It is thus perhaps no coincidence that Myrdal in the 1930s became one of the architects of the Social Democratic "People's Home". During most of the 1920s, he stayed away from politics. He studied for Cassel but soon became critical of the liberal generation of Cassel, Heckscher and Bagge. In 1929–1930, he spent time in the United States as a Rockefeller fellow and met with leading institutionalists like Wesley Mitchell, John Commons and John Maurice Clark. According to his own historiography, he and his wife

---

[17]B. Carlson, "Bagge, Lindahl och nationalinkomsten: Om National Income of Sweden 1861–1930", Lund: *Meddelande från Ekonomisk-historiska institutionen*, no. 27 (1982); P. G. Andreen and G. Boalt, "Bagge får tacka Rockefeller", Stockholms universitet – Socialhögskolan: *Rapport i socialt arbete*, no. 30 (1987); and E. Craver, "Gösta Bagge, The Rockefeller Foundation, and Empirical Social Science Research in Sweden, 1924–1940", in *The Stockholm School of Economics Revisited*, ed. L. Jonung (Cambridge: Cambridge University Press, 1991).

[18]E. Wadensjö, "The Committee on Unemployment and the Stockholm School", in *The Stockholm School of Economics Revisited*, ed. L. Jonung (Cambridge: Cambridge University Press, 1991).

[19]Some sources on Bagge: T. Aronson, *Gösta Bagges politiska tänkande: En studie i 1900-talets svenska konservatism* (Stockholm: Norstedts Juridik, 1993); P. G. Andreen, *Gösta Bagge som samhällsbyggare: Kommunalpolitiker – Socialpolitiker – Ecklesiastikminister* (Stockholm: Almqvist & Wiksell International, 1999).

Alva became democratic socialists after having been confronted with Americas social problems; he joined the Social Democratic Party in 1932. Two years later, he succeeded Cassel as professor of economics at Stockholm University. During most of the 1930s, it was full steam ahead for Myrdal as a member of the *Riksdag* and of several government commissions. In 1944, he became chairman of the powerful commission for post-war planning and when the Social Democrats in 1945 formed government he was appointed Minister for Trade and Commerce, but resigned this post in 1947. Myrdal became, alongside John Kenneth Galbraith, the world's most renowned institutionalist economist. He claimed he had become institutionalist all by himself, despite his early acquaintance with US institutionalism.[20] Anyway, he used this outlook in his magnum opuses *American Dilemma* (1944) and *Asian Drama* (1968).[21]

- Bertil Ohlin (1899–1979) was a "whizz-kid" who got his Bachelor's degree at 18, his Ph.D. at 25 and immediately thereafter became professor at Copenhagen University. He returned to Sweden and succeeded Heckscher as professor at the Stockholm School of Economics in 1929. The theorem he formulated in his dissertation[22] and his

---

[20]Myrdal did not appreciate the American institutionalists of his own time since he figured that they had not upheld the radical, Marxist-oriented stance of Veblen, but moved in a conservative direction. See G. Myrdal, "Kring den praktiska nationalekonomiens problematik", *Ekonomisk Tidskrift* 33(2) (1931).

[21]G. Myrdal, *An American Dilemma: The Negro Problem and Modern Democracy* (New York: Harper & Brothers, 1944); *Asian Drama: An Inquiry into the Poverty of Nations* (New York: Pantheon, 1968). Some English-language sources on Myrdal: E. Lundberg, "Gunnar Myrdal's Contribution to Economic Theory", *Swedish Journal of Economics* 76(4) (1974); J. Angresano, *Gunnar Myrdal's Intellectual Development as an Institutional Economist* (PhD diss., University of Tennessee, 1981); A. Carlson, *The Swedish Experiment in Family Politics: The Myrdals and the Interwar Population Crisis* (New Brunswick and London: Transaction Publishers, 1990); G. Dostaler, "An Assessment of Gunnar Myrdal's Early Work in Economics", *Journal of the History of Economic Thought* 12(Fall) (1990); W. A. Jackson, *Gunnar Myrdal and America's Conscience: Social Engineering and Racial Liberalism, 1938–1987* (Chapel Hill, NC: University of North Carolina Press, 1990); G. Dostaler, D. Ethier, and L. Lepage (eds.), *Gunnar Myrdal and His Works* (Montreal: Harvest House Ltd, 1992); W. J. Barber, *Gunnar Myrdal: An Intellectual Biography* (Basingstoke, UK and New York: Palgrave Macmillan, 2008); and B. Carlson, "Gunnar Myrdal", *Econ Journal Watch* 10(3) (2013).

[22]B. Ohlin, *Handelns teori* (Stockholm: Centraltryckeriet, 1924).

book on *Interregional and International Trade* (1933),[23] inspired by Heckscher's 1919 article, is often seen as his most important scientific contribution. He advanced along similar lines as Keynes and presented his analysis in a report to the Committee on Unemployment.[24] When Keynes' *General Theory* appeared in 1936, Ohlin understood that the theoretical advances accomplished in Stockholm ran the risk of being marginalized and he presented the concept of the Stockholm school in two articles in *Economic Journal*.[25] Ohlin started out as a classical liberal, moved in a social liberal direction after 1925 and became allied to Myrdal in the early 1930s. In 1934, he became chairman of the Liberal Party's youth organization and in 1938 took a seat in the *Riksdag*. In 1944, he became leader of the Liberal Party and Minister of Trade in the government of national unity. When the Social Democrats formed their own government in 1945 and launched a campaign for economic planning, Ohlin turned obstinate. He was thus to be found on different sides in the debates on economic planning in the 1930s and 1940s.[26]

Three of these five economists wrote in daily newspapers on a regular basis. Cassel wrote about 1500 pieces (mostly editorials) in *Svenska Dagbladet* (Conservative) between 1903 and 1944, whereof 430 of them between 1929 and 1939 with a peak of 47 in 1934. Ohlin wrote about 1200 pieces (a mix of editorials and articles) in *Stockholms-Tidningen* (Liberal) between 1925 and 1960; 600 between 1929 and 1939 with a peak of 83 articles in 1933. Heckscher wrote almost

---

[23]B. Ohlin, *Interregional and International Trade* (Cambridge: Harvard University Press, 1933).

[24]B. Ohlin, *Penningpolitik, offentliga arbeten, subventioner och tullar som medel mot arbetslöshet: Bidrag till expansionens teori* (Stockholm: P. A. Norstedt & Söner, 1934) (SOU 1934:12).

[25]B. Ohlin "Some Notes on the Stockholm Theory of Savings and Investment I-II", *Economic Journal* 47(185) (1937) and 47(186) (1937).

[26]Some English-language sources on Ohlin: H. Brems, "Bertil Ohlin's Contributions to Economic Theory", Urbana-Champaign: *BEBR Faculty Working Paper*, no. 1305 (1986); M. Blaug (ed.), *Pioneers in Economics: Bertil Ohlin (1899–1979)* (Aldershot: Edward Elgar, 1992); R. Findlay, L. Jonung, and M. Lundahl (eds.), *Bertil Ohlin: A Centennial Celebration (1899–1999)* (Cambridge, MA: MIT Press, 2002); N. Berggren, "Bertil Ohlin", *Econ Journal Watch* 10(3) (2013); and Lundahl, *Seven Figures*. A section on Ohlin and planning can be found in S.-E. Larsson, *Bertil Ohlin* (Stockholm: Atlantis, 1996).

300 articles in *Dagens Nyheter* (Liberal) between 1921 and 1949; 100 between 1929 and 1939. Bagge and Myrdal wrote sparingly for newspapers.[27]

Relations between the "big five" were strained for both ideological and personal reasons. Heckscher was particularly touchy. His relation with Cassel had been sour for a long time although they were ideological brothers-in-arms, mostly because he disliked Cassel's self-assured behaviour. His friendship with Bagge gradually deteriorated and in the 1930s he clashed, as our story will show, with Ohlin and Myrdal, not least over the planning issue, in a way that left scars forever. Cassel had similar ideological disputes with Ohlin and Myrdal, but they did not end in personal animosity.[28]

A few other economists occasionally intervened in the debate: David Davidson (1854–1942) was professor of economics and finance at Uppsala University 1890–1919 and editor of the Swedish economic journal *Ekonomisk Tidskrift* 1899–1938. He wrote regularly in this journal but held no high profile in current public debates.[29] Sven Brisman (1881–1953) was professor of economics and banking at the Stockholm School of Economics 1917–1946. He wrote fairly regularly in newspapers, but his articles are hard to find.[30] Karin Kock (1891–1976) was associate professor of economics at Stockholm University in the 1930s. She was appointed full professor in 1945 and government Minister 1947–1949. Kock was not very outspoken in the 1930s debate on

---

[27]See B. Carlson and L. Jonung, "Gustav Cassels artiklar i Svenska Dagbladet: Register 1903–1944", Lund: *Meddelande från Ekonomisk-historiska institutionen*, no. 62 (1989); B. Carlson, H. Orrje, and E. Wadensjö, *Ohlins artiklar: Register över Bertil Ohlins artiklar i skandinaviska tidningar och tidskrifter 1919–1979* (Stockholm: Institutet för social forskning, 2000); *Eli F. Heckschers bibliografi 1897–1949* (Stockholm: Ekonomisk-historiska institutet, 1950); Aronson, *Gösta Bagges politiska tänkande*; and H. Bohrn, *Gunnar Myrdal: A Bibliography, 1919–1976* (Stockholm: Kungliga Biblioteket, 1976).

[28]Bagge and Myrdal seem to have been inclined to upset each other's plans for reasons of personal rivalry. See Andreen, *Gösta Bagge som samhällsbyggare*; and Lundahl, *Seven Figures in the History of Swedish Economic Thought*.

[29]C. G. Uhr, *Economic Doctrines of David Davidson* (Berkeley: University of California Press, 1975).

[30]Brisman wrote in *Göteborgs Handels och Sjöfartstidning* (GHT), based in Gothenburg. However, there is no Brisman bibliography and the newspaper has not yet been digitized.

planning, although she used the term off and on, but she would be more so in the 1940s debate.[31] Gustaf Åkerman (1888–1959) was professor of economics and sociology at Gothenburg University 1931–1953 and his younger brother Johan Åkerman (1896–1982) was associate professor from 1932 and professor 1943–1961 at Lund University.[32]

Other economists of the older generation,[33] hardly to be heard in the debate, were Emil Sommarin (1874–1955), professor in Lund, admirer of Adam Smith and Social Democrat but "no party man" and "far from a planned economy theoretician"[34]; Fritz Brock (1877–1956), an eccentric professor in Uppsala[35]; and Erik Lindahl (1891–1969), in the 1930s professor at Gothenburg School of Economics and Lund University and member of the Stockholm school, working on a general dynamic theory involving planning at the micro level.[36] Gunnar Westin Silverstolpe (1891–1975) was professor at the Gothenburg School of Business Economics in the 1920s and early 1930s; he was particularly known as a popularizer of economics.[37]

The younger members of the Stockholm school—Dag Hammarskjöld (1905–1961), Erik Lundberg (1907–1987) and Ingvar Svennilson (1908–1972)—were surely interested in economic planning but not

---

[31]Kock was not involved in the theoretical work pursued by the Stockholm school economists. Her biographer, however, thinks that she can be seen as belonging to the "school" since "she shared the economic-political opinions of her colleagues and their overall radical view of society". See K. Niskanen, *Karriär i männens värld: Nationalekonomen och feministen Karin Kock* (Stockholm: SNS Förlag, 2007), 105–106. See also C. Jonung and L. Jonung, "Karin Kock 1891–1976", in *Svenska nationalekonomer under 400 år*, ed. C. Jonung and A.-C. Ståhlberg (Stockholm: Dialogos, 2014).

[32]H. Hegeland, "Gustaf Åkerman", and E. Dahmén, "Johan Åkerman", in *Svenska nationalekonomer under 400 år*, ed. C. Jonung and A.-C. Ståhlberg (Stockholm: Dialogos, 2014).

[33]Two leading figures in the older generation passed away before the debate took off: Knut Wicksell (1851–1926) and Gustaf Steffen (1864–1929).

[34]C. Welinder, "Emil Sommarin 1874–1955", in *Svenska nationalekonomer under 400 år*, ed. C. Jonung and A.-C. Ståhlberg (Stockholm. Dialogos, 2014), 189, 191.

[35]E. Wadensjö, *Fritz Brock: An Eccentric Economist* (Stockholm: Swedish Institute for Social Research, 1994).

[36]J. Petersson, *Erik Lindahl och Stockholmsskolans dynamiska metod* (Lund: Lund Economic Studies 39, 1987).

[37]J. Lönnroth, "Gunnar Westin Silverstolpe", in *Svenska nationalekonomer under 400 år*, ed. C. Jonung and A.-C. Ståhlberg (Stockholm: Dialogos, 2014).

much visible in the 1930s planning debate. The title of Svennilson's 1938 doctoral dissertation was "Economic Planning"; it was a theoretical piece on corporate planning.[38] He became a diligent middle-of-the-road participant in the 1940s debate on economic planning.[39] Nonetheless, economists probably played a less prominent role in the 1940s compared to the 1930s. Cassel died in 1945 and Bagge, Ohlin and Myrdal were full-time politicians and had to consider party lines when they said or wrote something. Heckscher, however, was still in fighting spirit and free from party ties.[40]

Ernst Wigforss (1881–1977) will also play a role in our story. He was the leading Social Democratic ideologist of the time. Although he was a politician, educated within the humanities (with a doctorate in Scandinavian languages), he was (as mentioned in Chapter 1) at the forefront of developments within economics alongside the economists of the Stockholm school.

References

Andreen, P. G. *Gösta Bagge som samhällsbyggare: Kommunalpolitiker – Socialpolitiker – Ecklesiastikminister.* Stockholm: Almqvist & Wiksell International, 1999.

Andreen, P. G., and G. Boalt. "Bagge får tacka Rockefeller". Stockholms universitet – Socialhögskolan: *Rapport i socialt arbete*, no. 30 (1987).

Angresano, J. *Gunnar Myrdal's Intellectual Development as an Institutional Economist.* PhD diss., University of Tennessee, 1981.

Aronson, T. *Gösta Bagges politiska tänkande: En studie i 1900-talets svenska konservatism.* Stockholm: Norstedts Juridik, 1993.

---

[38]I. Svennilson, *Ekonomisk planering: Teoretiska studier* (Uppsala: Almqvist & Wiksells Tryckeri AB, 1938).

[39]B. Carlson and M. Lundahl, "Ingvar Svennilson on Economic Planning in War and Peace", *History of Economic Ideas* 25(2) (2017).

[40]The most internationally renowned of the above-mentioned economists appear as entries in *The New Palgrave* (in alphabetical order): Cassel, Davidson, Hammarskjöld, Heckscher, Lindahl, Lundberg, Myrdal, Ohlin, Svennilson and the Åkerman brothers. See *The New Palgrave of Economics*, ed. J. Eatwell, M. Milgrave, and P. Newman (London: Macmillan, 1987).

Bagge, G. *Arbetslönens reglering genom sammanslutningar.* Stockholm: AB Nordiska Bokhandeln, 1917.

Barber, W. J. *Gunnar Myrdal: An Intellectual Biography.* Basingstoke, UK and New York: Palgrave Macmillan, 2008.

Berggren, N. "Bertil Ohlin". *Econ Journal Watch* 10(3) (2013): 532–536.

Blaug, M. (ed.). *Pioneers in Economics: Bertil Ohlin (1899–1979).* Aldershot: Edward Elgar, 1992.

Bohrn, H. *Gunnar Myrdal: A Bibliography, 1919–1976.* Stockholm: Kungliga Biblioteket, 1976.

Brems, H. "Bertil Ohlin's Contributions to Economic Theory". Urbana-Champaign: *BEBR Faculty Working Paper*, no. 1305 (1986).

Brems, H. "Gustav Cassel Revisited". *History of Political Economy* 21(2) (1989): 165–178.

Carlson, A. *The Swedish Experiment in Family Politics: The Myrdals and the Interwar Population Crisis.* New Brunswick and London: Transaction Publishers, 1990.

Carlson, B. "Bagge, Lindahl och nationalinkomsten: Om National Income of Sweden 1861–1930". Lund: *Meddelande från Ekonomisk-historiska institutionen*, no. 27 (1982).

Carlson, B. "Gösta Bagge's American Lessons". *Scandinavian Economic History Review* 39(2) (1991): 29–41.

Carlson, B. *The State as a Monster: Gustav Cassel and Eli Heckscher on the Role and Growth of the State.* Lanham: University Press of America, 1994.

Carlson, B. "Who Was Most World-Famous—Cassel or Keynes? *The Economist* as Yardstick". *Journal of the History of Economic Thought* 31(4) (2009): 519–530.

Carlson, B. "Gunnar Myrdal". *Econ Journal Watch* 10(3) (2013): 507–520.

Carlson, B. "Eli Heckscher's Ideological Migration Toward Market Liberalism". *Econ Journal Watch* 13(1) (2016): 75–99.

Carlson, B., and L. Jonung. "Gustav Cassels artiklar i Svenska Dagbladet: Register 1903–1944". Lund: *Meddelande från Ekonomisk-historiska institutionen*, no. 62 (1989).

Carlson, B., and L. Jonung. "Knut Wicksell, Gustav Cassel, Eli Heckscher, Bertil Ohlin and Gunnar Myrdal on the Role of the Economist in Public Debate". *Econ Journal Watch* 3(3) (2006): 511–550.

Carlson, B., and M. Lundahl. "Ingvar Svennilson on Economic Planning in War and Peace". *History of Economic Ideas* 25(2) (2017): 115–138.

Carlson, B., H. Orrje, and E. Wadensjö. *Ohlins artiklar: Register över Bertil Ohlins artiklar i skandinaviska tidningar och tidskrifter 1919–1979.* Stockholm: Institutet för social forskning, 2000.

Cassel, G. *Socialpolitik.* Stockholm: Hugo Gebers Förlag, 1902.

Cassel, G. *Theoretische Sozialökonomie.* Leipzig: C.F. Winter, 1918.

Cassel, G. *The Theory of Social Economy.* London: T. Fisher Unwin, 1923.

Cassel, G. *I förnuftets tjänst,* vols. 1–2. Stockholm: Natur och Kultur, 1940–1941.

Craver, E. "Gösta Bagge, the Rockefeller Foundation, and Empirical Social Science Research in Sweden, 1924–1940". In *The Stockholm School of Economics Revisited,* edited by L. Jonung, 79–97. Cambridge: Cambridge University Press, 1991.

Dahmén, E. "Johan Åkerman". In *Svenska nationalekonomer under 400 år,* edited by C. Jonung and A.-C. Ståhlberg, 304–316. Stockholm: Dialogos, 2014.

Dostaler, G. "An Assessment of Gunnar Myrdal's Early Work in Economics". *Journal of the History of Economic Thought* 12(Fall) (1990): 197–221.

Dostaler, G., D. Ethier, and L. Lepage (eds.). *Gunnar Myrdal and His Works.* Montreal: Harvest House, 1992.

Eli F. Heckschers bibliografi 1897–1949. Stockholm: Ekonomisk-historiska institutet, 1950.

Findlay, R., R. G. H. Henriksson, H. Lindgren, and M. Lundahl (eds.). *Eli Heckscher, International Trade and Economic History.* Cambridge, MA and London: MIT Press, 2006.

Findlay, R., L. Jonung, and M. Lundahl (eds.). *Bertil Ohlin: A Centennial Celebration (1899–1999).* Cambridge, MA: MIT Press, 2002.

Hasselberg, Y. *Industrisamhällets förkunnare: Eli Heckscher, Arthur Montgomery, Bertil Boëthius och svensk ekonomisk historia 1920–1950.* Hedemora/Möklinta: Gidlunds Förlag, 2007.

Heckscher, E. "Utrikeshandelns verkan på inkomstfördelningen: Några teoretiska grundlinjer". Nationalekonomiska studier tillägnade professor David Davidson. *Ekonomisk Tidskrift* 21(2) (1919): 1–32.

Heckscher, E. *Gammal och ny ekonomisk liberalism.* Stockholm: P. A. Norstedt & Söner, 1921.

Heckscher, E. *Mercantilism I-II.* London: Allen & Unwin, 1935.

Heckscher, E. *Sveriges ekonomiska historia från Gustav Vasa I-II.* Stockholm: Albert Bonniers Förlag, 1935–1936.

Heckscher, E. "The Effect of Foreign Trade on the Distribution of Income". In *Heckscher-Ohlin Trade Theory,* edited by H. Flam and J. Flanders, 36–69. Cambridge, MA and London: MIT Press, 1991.

Heckscher, E. *Om staten, liberalismen och den ekonomiska politiken: Texter i urval av Kurt Wickman.* Stockholm: Timbro, 2000.

Hegeland, H. "Gustaf Åkerman". In *Svenska nationalekonomer under 400 år*, edited by C. Jonung and A.-C. Ståhlberg, 242–252. Stockholm: Dialogos, 2014.

Henriksson, R. G. H. "Eli F. Heckscher: The Economic Historian as Economist". In *The History of Swedish Economic Thought*, edited by B. Sandelin, 141–167. London and New York: Routledge, 1991.

Jackson, W. A. *Gunnar Myrdal and America's Conscience: Social Engineering and Racial Liberalism, 1938–1987*. Chapel Hill, NC: University of North Carolina Press, 1990.

Jonung, C., and L. "Karin Kock 1891–1976". In *Svenska nationalekonomer under 400 år*, edited by C. Jonung and A.-C. Ståhlberg, 287–303. Stockholm: Dialogos, 2014.

Jonung, C., and A.-C. Ståhlberg (eds.). *Svenska nationalekonomer under 400 år*. Stockholm: Dialogos, 2014.

Lönnroth, J. "Gunnar Westin Silverstolpe". In *Svenska nationalekonomer under 400 år*, edited by C. Jonung and A.-C. Ståhlberg, 269–286. Stockholm: Dialogos, 2014.

Lundahl, M. *Seven Figures in the History of Swedish Economic Thought: Knut Wicksell, Eli Heckscher, Bertil Ohlin, Torsten Gårdlund, Sven Rydelfelt, Staffan Burenstam Linder and Jamie Behar*. Houndmills, Basingstoke, Hampshire: Palgrave Macmillan, 2015.

Lundberg, E. "The Influence of Gustav Cassel on Economic Doctrine and Policy". *Skandinaviska Banken Quarterly Review* 48(1) (1967): 1–6.

Lundberg, E. "Gunnar Myrdal's Contribution to Economic Theory". *Swedish Journal of Economics* 76(4) (1974): 472–478.

Magnusson, L. "Gustav Cassel, Popularizer and Enigmatic Walrasian". In *The History of Swedish Economic Thought*, edited by B. Sandelin, 122–140. London and New York: Routledge, 1991.

Montgomery, A. "Gustav Cassel, 1866–1945". *Economic Journal* 57(228) (1947): 532–542.

Myrdal, G. "Kring den praktiska nationalekonomiens problematik". *Ekonomisk Tidskrift* 33(2) (1931): 41–81.

Myrdal, G. *An American Dilemma: The Negro Problem and Modern Democracy*. New York: Harper & Brothers, 1944.

Myrdal, G. *Asian Drama: An Inquiry into the Poverty of Nations*. New York: Pantheon, 1968.

Niskanen, K. *Karriär i männens värld: Nationalekonomen och feministen Karin Kock*. Stockholm: SNS Förlag, 2007.

Ohlin, B. *Handelns teori*. Stockholm: Centraltryckeriet, 1924.

Ohlin, B. *Interregional and International Trade.* Cambridge: Harvard University Press, 1933.

Ohlin, B. *Penningpolitik, offentliga arbeten, subventioner och tullar som medel mot arbetslöshet: Bidrag till expansionens teori.* Stockholm: P. A. Norstedt & Söner, 1934 (SOU 1934:12).

Ohlin, B. "Some Notes on the Stockholm Theory of Savings and Investment I-II". *Economic Journal* 47(185) (March 1937): 53–69 and 47(186) (June 1937): 221–240.

Pålsson-Syll, L. "Cassel and Revealed Preference Theory". *History of Political Economy* 25(3) (1993): 499–514.

Petersson, J. *Erik Lindahl och Stockholmsskolans dynamiska metod.* Lund: Lund Economic Studies 39, 1987.

Samuelson, P. "Gustav Cassel's Scientific Innovations: Claims and Realities". *History of Political Economy* 25(3) (1993): 515–527.

Svennilson, I. *Ekonomisk planering: Teoretiska studier.* Uppsala: Almqvist & Wiksells Tryckeri AB, 1938.

The New Palgrave of Economics, edited by J. Eatwell, M. Milgrave, and P. Newman. London: Macmillan, 1987.

Uhr, C. G. *Economic Doctrines of David Davidson.* Berkeley: University of California Press, 1975.

Uhr, C. G. "Eli F. Heckscher, 1879–1952, and His Treatise on Mercantilism Revisited". *Economy and History* 23(1) (1980): 3–39.

Wadensjö, E. "Gösta Bagge: An Entrepreneur in Swedish Economics". In *Swedish Economic Thought: Explorations and Advances*, edited by L. Jonung, 109–124. London and New York: Routledge, 1993.

Wadensjö, E. *Fritz Brock: An Eccentric Economist.* Stockholm: Swedish Institute for Social Research, 1994.

Welinder, C. "Emil Sommarin 1874–1955". In *Svenska nationalekonomer under 400 år*, edited by C. Jonung and A.-C. Ståhlberg, 184–192. Stockholm: Dialogos, 2014.

4

Economists in the Swedish Debate

Abstract During the 1920s, the Swedish debate on the role of the state in the economy was lively. The fight over planning began in earnest in 1930, when the Conservative government introduced a "milling obligation" which Eli Heckscher branded as "economic planning with no plan", after the pattern of Soviet Russia. The New Deal caught the attention in mid-1933 and was particularly scrutinized by Bertil Ohlin. In early 1934, when the Social Democrats revealed their intention to increase the influence of the state over economic life in spite of the economic recovery, the planning debate went into high gear. When Gunnar Myrdal succeeded Gustav Cassel as professor of economics at Stockholm University, he emphasized the necessity of central economic planning. Cassel, in a lecture in London, warned that cumulative government interventions would end in dictatorship. Heckscher, in the Economic Society, attacked his younger colleagues as "apostles of the planned economy". Myrdal and Ohlin countered that interventions were needed to avoid major dangers. The next major battle, with Heckscher and Ohlin as antagonists, took place when economists from the Nordic countries in 1935 convened in Oslo. In 1936, Ohlin summarized his ideas on "framework planning" in a book on "Free or Directed Economy".

© The Author(s) 2018   **47**
B. Carlson, *Swedish Economists in the 1930s Debate
on Economic Planning*, Palgrave Studies in Economic History,
https://doi.org/10.1007/978-3-030-03700-0_4

When John Maynard Keynes' *General Theory* appeared, Cassel and Heckscher claimed it was all but general, whereas Ohlin attempted to establish that the younger generation of Stockholm economists had attacked the same problems as Keynes independently of him.

Keywords Swedish economists · Economic planning · Government interventions · Dictatorship · Framework planning

The Swedish Social Democratic programmes of the early 1900s spoke of replacing "planless production" with production planned in accordance with "the real needs of society". Socialization and economic planning were in those days regarded as Siamese twins and no plans for operating them separately were launched. This is not to say that ideas for a shift of emphasis from socialization to economic planning did not exist long before the 1930s. Gustav Cassel conjectured that the Social Democratic movement would come to regard socialization less as a sacred principle and more as one element among others in practical policy. He cited an article by the political economist and Social Democrat Gustaf Steffen, in which the latter declared that society must have the right and the power to make sure that privately owned means of production were being used in the most efficient manner possible from the national economic standpoint. "Such a transformation of socialism's ideological content in a practical direction should of course be greeted with joy by all those who oppose socialism", wrote Cassel.[1]

Certain features of economic development were such as to trigger speculation along planned economy lines. The private sector of the economy seemed to be marked by a trend towards monopoly and more of organization of corporate life. The experience from WWI raised questions concerning the state's capacity to direct a capitalist economy—Ernst Wigforss has pointed out that economic planning was "a term frequently used in the debates that followed World War I".[2] Nonetheless, it seems as if the talk of economic planning began in the mid-1920s. Our story will begin in 1925.

---

[1]G. Cassel, "Hvad är socialism?" *Svenska Dagbladet*, October 20, 1910.
[2]E. Wigforss, "Ideologiska linjer i praktisk politik", *Tiden* 59(9) (1967): 530.

From Russia with Chaos

Bertil Ohlin seems to have been the first economist to intercept the new signals from British radical Liberals, among them Keynes, putting forward proposals on how to stabilize economic life through organized cooperation between different interests. Ohlin noted that these proposals had little in common with Manchester liberalism—they rather indicated "a socialism of a completely new kind"—and he interpreted the term used by the British ("coordinated efforts") as "planned cooperation". Ohlin wished to see something similar in Sweden.[3]

In 1925, Eli Heckscher attended the bicentennial celebration of the Russian Academy of Science. In contrast to many other Western visitors, who undertook pilgrimage to the Soviet Union to behold the future of mankind, he was not impressed. He reported about his visit in a series of articles in *Dagens Nyheter*. In his first article, Heckscher gave a vivid picture of Saint Petersburg/Leningrad, which seemed to mirror "the bankruptcy of communism". "The word decay is written in large letters all over the city". He, however, admitted that this was much due to the rise of Moscow as the new Russian capital.[4]

In his final article, Heckscher discussed economic planning since one "basic idea within the Communist Russian order is to replace the so-called anarchic system of free competition with 'planned economy'".[5] He conveyed his impressions from a meeting where a few invited economists had been informed about Gosplan, this "mighty authority" with 13 members, most of them scientists not affiliated to the Communist Party.[6] They had at their disposal a host of experts producing large quantities of statistics. However, it was difficult to judge if the statistics pointing to the future were preliminary calculations or

---

[3]B. Ohlin, "Den nyaste socialismen", *Stockholms-Tidningen*, April 26, 1925.

[4]E. Heckscher, "Intryck från Ryssland I: Petersburg och Moskva", *Dagens Nyheter*, September 21, 1925.

[5]E. Heckscher, "Intryck från Ryssland VI: 'Planhushållning' och förnöjsamhet", *Dagens Nyheter*, October 9, 1925.

[6]Five years later, in 1930, it was "being purged" when "political qualifications replaced technical ones for staffing Gosplan". See P. Temin, "Soviet and Nazi Economic Planning in the 1930s", *Economic History Review* 44(4) (1991): 574.

prescriptions. Gosplan showed good intentions to bring some order to Russia. Nonetheless, to a Western observer, the country gave a "general impression of planlessness". Anyone who had done business with the Soviet regime knew that "it is the unexpected that happens". "The leadership has faltered from one extreme to the other, determined grain prices which could not be upheld, thrown unpredictable quantities of goods into the market, for some time unleashed private commerce and then suddenly ruined it by choking its credit, etc.". This planlessness probably had roots in the old imperial autocracy and was not caused by any unwillingness by the regime to engage scholars and experts. However:

> It is difficult to ignore that the communist system itself is to a large extent part of the planlessness, although its goal is the opposite. Within the economic field you do not in reality get far with an ever so eminent expertise if you cannot use the expert which in French is labelled "tout le monde", in other words: free price formation. At least, I think most economists would agree that not even the best statistics – which perhaps do not exist in Russia – would enable them to predict the future interplay between the thousands of forces which in combination shape the economic context.

However, might there in Russia be some other objective concerned with spiritual needs and different from the Western one, aimed at satisfying material needs? This option was dismissed by Heckscher for two reasons: Firstly, the Soviet regime could not know much about people's spiritual needs since it was authoritarian and stifled the freedom of speech. Secondly, communism was an imported doctrine not rooted in Russia. Still, if Russia was heading for a "harmonious and static" condition, one could perhaps see this as some kind of progress from a higher perspective than the material one. However, a static condition must rest upon a fairly static population and this was not the case in Russia. Heckscher concluded his article by pointing to the Russian lawlessness:

> Even if some fascist or communist philosophers would want to prove that such conditions are suitable for many people – which perhaps might not be impossible – anyone who thinks that the human mission is free spiritual development within the rule of law cannot accept this. From

such an understanding present Russian conditions amount to a barbarism which one must not accept.

The following year, Heckscher came back to the planning theme. "Throughout the world at the present time, discussions are going on as to what conclusions are suggested by the experiences of wartime as regards the feasibility of 'economic planning'", Heckscher observed, and he went on to say that the war experience had shown the state unable to cope with its most important task, maintaining a stable currency. Heckscher described the opinion at which he had arrived during the war concerning the state's capacity for management as being "that even a government possessing both insight and the will to act correctly has a very difficult task in selecting the right instruments, to the extent that an exceedingly unenlightened public opinion is striving in another direction".[7]

During the 1920s, Cassel was a relentless critic of everything with a smack of socialism, including economic planning. Early in 1926, he wrote:

According to the holy books the basic error of the present social order is its planlessness: in contrast to the socialist society there is no top management which guarantees that the productive forces are always and everywhere correctly aligned. With a favorite expression, production is "anarchic" and the result must be perpetual deficiencies in the correspondence between the supply of labor and the demand for the products of labour, i.e. alternately scarcity of products and unemployment. Socialism, naturally in this primitive analysis, forgets the historical contribution that liberalism has made by demonstrating that a top management – which mercantilism put all its faith into – is redundant and can never manage the task assigned to it, but can to immeasurable advantage be replaced by the interest of individual entrepreneurs, which must always

---

[7]E. Heckscher, "Inledande översikt", in *Bidrag till Sveriges ekonomiska och sociala historia under och efter världskriget*, ed. E. Heckscher (Stockholm: P. A. Norstedt & Söner, 1926), 24–26. When this introduction was translated into English as E. Heckscher "Sweden in the World War. Part I. General Survey", in *Sweden, Norway, Denmark and Iceland in the World War*, ed. E. Heckscher et al. (New Haven: Yale University Press, 1930), the section on planned economy was not included.

coincide with the most accurate correspondence between production and the desire of consumption. [...] The socialist doctrine that capital formation in a capitalist society would restrain consumption and thus cause a more or less permanent over-production is from the very beginning a false idea [...].[8]

Later that year, Cassel designated socialism as "the greatest charlatanry of our time". A socialist society, with an authoritative management of the economy according to the public interest, could never accept trade unions, with their particular interests, nor the freedom of workers to move between different locations and trades. It would also open the door to important leading positions for people who "have not been able to advance in tough economic competition but have chosen to rise to the heights of society using a fluent tongue and populist phrase-mongering".[9]

Cassel eventually collected a series of articles in a book called "Socialism or Progress". In a postscript, he accused socialists of cultivating a dogmatic faith "which is expressed in an absurd, sometimes almost superstitious, overestimation of government ownership, government management and government control in all spheres of the national economy".[10] He pointed to the Russian example. Soviet Russia had proved itself unfit as a social-economic system since it could not itself mobilize capital and lacked technical, organizational and commercial management. "An economic system, incapable of taking care of such management in a satisfactory way is obviously useless".[11] If the whole world followed in Russia's footsteps, it would be the end of all technological and organizational progress and the beginning of an era of hopeless poverty.

---

[8]G. Cassel, "Dogmatik och verklighet", *Svenska Dagbladet*, February 26, 1926.

[9]G. Cassel, "Vår tids största charlataneri", *Svenska Dagbladet*, December 5, 1926.

[10]G. Cassel, *Socialism eller framåtskridande* (Stockholm: P. A. Norstedt & Söners Förlag, 1928), 239.

[11]Ibid., 240. Wigforss, in a lengthy review of the book, tried to apply a rather good-humoured tone, but was apparently upset since he argued that Cassel had accused "those who are worst off" of "socialist greediness, ignorance and envy". He also admitted that Cassel's "relentless repetition strains the nerves somewhat". See E. Wigforss, "Professor Cassel och socialismen", *Tiden* 21(2) (1929): 66, 78.

Liberalism at the Crossroads

In late 1927, Ohlin published two articles titled "Liberalism at the crossroads". He declared that liberalism was in a state of crisis. New issues were on the agenda, and new mentalities had developed. "The belief that everything will be fine if society just refrains from intervention and relies on free initiative has been wrecked". The economy was no longer dominated by many independent and individually owned businesses but by big corporations managed by salaried officials. Competition had taken new directions as the importance of fixed capital had increased. During economic slumps, corporations were involved in either destructive competition or mergers, in both cases leading to monopoly. People's mentality had changed when economic growth slowed down and long-term unemployment unfolded. "*A planned organization, guaranteeing rationality and efficiency, instead of the laissez-faire system of the old society*, has become the order of the day. The demand for freedom has been moved out of the way by the demand for rationality".[12]

Liberalism was thus at a crossroad. In Ohlin's view, it could either cling to the freedom principle and attempt to put breaks on development—"such a policy is in principle *reactionary*"—or it could embrace an outlook accepting "the demand for a *planned organization even when this entails a restriction of freedom*". Liberalism must choose. Any attempt to sit on two chairs would end up in between them. "This is the real political divide, which is usually designated as *left* and *right*, progressive or conservative". It was necessary to take a stand on issues like monopolies, labour market organizations and income distribution. When treating these and other problems, a dividing line must be drawn between those who wished for public authorities to keep hands off and those who wished to see them contribute to organization according to plan. Ohlin cautioned against the naïve idea that public entities could do everything better than private businesses striving for profit, but his final words were harsh: "Between the old liberal view, unappreciative of

---

[12]B. Ohlin, "Liberalismen vid skiljovägen", *Stockholms-Tidningen*, December 27, 1927.

the economic demands of our time, and the neoliberal one, demanding that these problems be solved along rational lines, there can be no reconciliation or compromise".[13]

In early 1928, Heckscher reviewed the "Yellow Book", published by David Lloyd George and a committee including British economists like Keynes and H. D. Henderson. Heckscher attacked the idea of an economic "general staff" by referring to his impressions from his 1925 visit to Russia:

> The British proposal is, like its Russian role model, built upon the existence of all kinds of statistics which at present are lacking, but it displays a surprising optimism when one believes it possible, with this at best very blunt and fragile tool, to have a basis for the kind of regulation which economic life brings about by itself with the help of price formation.[14]

Had not eminent economists like Walter Thomas Layton (editor of *The Economist*) and Keynes been involved, one would, wrote Heckscher, "be tempted to suspect a lack of knowledge about fairly fundamental economic matters". Interestingly, Heckscher discussed what is nowadays labelled "market failure" versus "government failure":

> If we had at our disposal an omniscient and ever-wise governmental providence, it would be easy to design a society superior to the one led by in many cases shortsighted, ignorant and by improper private interests dominated business leaders; but when there are faulty people on both sides, the ruling must often turn out quite differently.

The idea of economic planning was marred by two particularly serious weaknesses. Firstly, public controls would put "a brake on the wheel"; it might even be that the bureaucracy would grow bigger than was the case under pure state operation. Secondly, the interest of consumers was more or less out of the picture. "What has been labelled liberal economic policy in the older sense, i.e. the regime of free competition, has

---

[13]B. Ohlin, "Liberalismen vid skiljovägen II", *Stockholms-Tidningen*, December 29, 1927.
[14]E. Heckscher, "Den icke-socialistiska framtidsstaten", *Dagens Nyheter*, February 17, 1928.

from the beginning to the end been aimed at putting economic activity in the service of consumption".

Wigforss reacted to the "Yellow Book" by underlining how close to socialism the British Liberals came and how different they were in this regard compared to their Swedish counterparts. The British Liberals had a programme for the immediate future, which the Swedish Social Democracy lacked: "we have general guidelines for our economic policy during a century, but not the concrete and practical design for a decade". The Britons regarded the state not as a necessary evil but as a useful tool for organizing society in the best way. They even proposed a *"government economic general staff"* and a "central board for directing large shares of society's savings".[15]

Ohlin also, under the title of "The future liberal state", devoted two articles to the "Yellow Book". Once again, he distanced himself from the old liberalism and its focus on personal freedom. The main task ahead was to investigate how government and private corporate bodies could make economic life more efficient and income distribution more just. "However, one must not draw the conclusion that the only solution is to completely abandon the existing system and put communism or socialism in its place". Private initiative should be used when it was beneficial and be restrained when it was not.[16] Ohlin designated both consistent state socialism and individual liberalism as absurd. He mentioned the proposal to set up an economic general staff and concluded by saying that the Yellow Book was "one of the most interesting economic and political documents which has seen the light of day for many years".[17]

A first clash between the older and younger generation of economists, mainly Heckscher and Myrdal, took place in the Political Economy Club (*Nationalekonomiska klubben*) in 1928. The club had been founded in 1916, on the initiative of Heckscher, to serve as a forum for discussion following Knut Wicksell's retirement. According to Rolf Henriksson, the clash had its origin in Keynes' pamphlet *The End*

---

[15]E. Wigforss, "Engelsk liberalism", *Tiden* 20(2) (1928): 66, 68.

[16]B. Ohlin, "Den liberala framtidsstaten I", *Stockholms-Tidningen*, March 27, 1928.

[17]B. Ohlin, "Den liberala framtidsstaten II", *Stockholms-Tidningen*, March 28, 1928.

of Laissez-Faire from 1926 and marked the starting point for Gunnar Myrdal's (1930) critical scrutiny of economic theory.[18] At the same time, Myrdal's opposition manifested itself at Bagge's seminar.[19]

Lloyd George's electoral promise in early 1929 to eradicate abnormal unemployment in Britain through loan-funded public works aroused a lot of attention. Heckscher was sceptic, recalling that Lloyd George had once promised to hang the Kaiser. However, this time, with Keynes behind him, his promise could perhaps be fulfilled.[20] Cassel on the one hand lauded the "positive character" of the promise, and, on the other hand, expressed concern over its promotion of huge public works. He focused on the crowding-out argument and did not touch upon planning issues more than—in passing—calling upon states to improve their own efficiency before thinking of intervening in private business life.[21] Ohlin was all the more positive, dismissed the crowding-out argument and discussed how such a programme could be carried out.[22] He also drew attention to Keynes' and Henderson's *Can Lloyd George Do It?* and agreed with Keynes that the crowding-out argument was nonsense.[23]

Two months after the crash on Wall Street, Cassel turned against Herbert Hoover's programme for "prosperity maintenance" in the US. To launch public works was a mistake based on a misunderstanding of the actual problem and on "an overestimate of the state's capacity". There was no crisis, just a slowdown in production, but the Federal Reserve had exerted an untimely tight monetary policy which could drag the whole world into depression.[24]

---

[18]R. G. H. Henriksson, "The Political Economy Club and the Stockholm School", in *The Stockholm School of Economics Revisited*, ed. L. Jonung (Cambridge: Cambridge University Press, 1991). The clash was originally revealed by Brisman in a review of Myrdal's book. See S. Brisman, "De unga nationalekonomernas revolt", *Göteborgs Handels- och Sjöfartstidning*, December 5, 1930. Myrdal's book: G. Myrdal, *Vetenskap och politik i nationalekonomien* (Stockholm: Norstedt, 1930), translated into *The Political Element in the Development of Economic Theory* (London: Routledge & Kegan Paul, 1953).

[19]P. G. Andreen, *Gösta Bagge som samhällsbyggare: Kommunalpolitiker – Socialpolitiker – Ecklesiastikminister* (Stockholm: Almqvist & Wiksell International, 1999).

[20]E. Heckscher, "Arbetslöshet och allmänna arbeten", *Dagens Nyheter*, March 26, 1929.

[21]G. Cassel, "Lloyd Georges valprogram," *Svenska Dagbladet*, April 10, 1929.

[22]B. Ohlin, "Lloyd George och arbetslösheten", *Stockholms-Tidningen*, April 18, 1929.

[23]B. Ohlin, "Valet och arbetslösheten i England", *Stockholms-Tidningen*, May 26, 1929.

[24]G. Cassel, "Statsmakt på avvägar", *Svenska Dagbladet*, December 31, 1929.

This, if anything, is a warning example of what happens when one indulges in the modern tendency to let state activity unnecessarily intervene in the economic field. The state assumes a task which does not belong to it, is tempted into a faulty management of one of its original tasks, the care of the monetary system, and thereby triggers a depression, which it then seeks to remedy through measures which also are beyond its proper field of activity and which can only make the situation worse.

Planning Without Plan

In early 1930, Cassel in a public lecture on "The degeneration of relief policy" attacked all kinds of "arbitrary" state interventions in price formation, whether in the shape of social, labour market or agricultural policy. This was in some quarters seen as a "declaration of war" against the Conservative Arvid Lindman government.[25] "The Conservative congregation feels like a herd without a shepherd", wrote a leading Liberal newspaper and continued: "One does not know what to think or whom to follow when the Conservative's foremost economic authority has abandoned the flag".[26] One more Liberal paper did not know what to think: "Such an unmitigated economic liberalism is perhaps easier to defend from a theoretical point of view than [it is for it] to survive under certain practical circumstances".[27]

Heckscher also clashed with both Conservative and Liberal interest groups. He opposed agricultural protectionism in a way which in some quarters rendered him the label "agriculture's enemy no. one".[28] When he launched an attack titled "Economic Planning", it was not aimed at any grand socialist experiment but at an obligation to mix a fixed proportion of home-grown with imported grain (which Cassel had

[25]Nya Dagligt Allehanda, "En krigsförklaring", *Nya Dagligt Allehanda*, February 15, 1930.

[26]Dagens Nyheter, "Fallet Cassel", *Dagens Nyheter*, February 18, 1930.

[27]Stockholms-Tidningen, "Professor Cassels framstöt", *Stockholms-Tidningen*, February 16, 1930. Cassel was comforted by the Swedish "tycoon" Marcus Wallenberg in a letter (February 29, 1930): "When one vindicates common sense and the inviolability of economic laws, one can take the barking from unreliable sources easy". Cassel's letters are at the Royal Library in Stockholm.

[28]A. Hirsch, *Minnen som dröjt kvar* (Stockholm: Lars Hökerbergs Bokförlag, 1953), 219.

also attacked in his lecture), introduced under the Conservative government. This "milling obligation" meant, according to Heckscher, "in all basic aspects 'planned economy' in Soviet Russian sense" and the board which was to administer the scheme was "a counterpart to the Russian Gosplan".[29] In another article on the same issue, Heckscher spoke of "'economic planning' with no plan, after the pattern familiar in Soviet Russia".[30] In yet another article, he pointed to the mercantilist ancestry of the proposition. In the sixteenth-century Britain, it was ordered that people be buried in woollen cloth in order to keep up the production of woollen manufactures.[31]

Heckscher also published an analysis of fascist and Bolshevik economic systems. In the fascist system, the foundations of the capitalist system, with its free consumption choice, were intact. The state merely intervened to prevent anything which could challenge its political hegemony. One ironic comment is topical in our time, when the media are under attack:

Many enlightened spirits have asked for how long the modern state would allow the lying and hounding which privately owned newspapers pursue in many countries. In fascist Italy their wishes have been fulfilled. A unison chorus of hundreds of parts to the glory of Mussolini is every day heard from newspapers all over Italy [...].[32]

In the Bolshevik system, the famous five-year plan was "a kind of borrowed Americanism; everything is intended to achieve 'the biggest in the world'". The main purpose was to limit consumption and promote an enormous capital formation. "Production has in this plan become an end in itself and thereby the issue is not about planning in an economic sense".[33]

---

[29]E. Heckscher, "Planhushållning", *Dagens Nyheter*, March 1, 1930.

[30]E. Heckscher, "Inmalningstvånget och dess konsekvenser", *Dagens Nyheter*, May 28, 1930.

[31]E. Heckscher, "Striden om jordbruket", *Svensk Tidskrift* 29 (1930).

[32]E. Heckscher, "Liberalism, fascism, bolsjevism som ekonomiska system", *Svensk Tidskrift* 29 (1930): 530. Cf. Tugwell, quoted from W. Schivelbusch, *Three New Deals: Reflections on Roosevelt's America, Mussolini's Italy, and Hitler's Germany, 1933–1939* (New York: Picador, 2006), 32: "Mussolini certainly has the same people opposed to him as F.D.R. has. But he has the press controlled so that they cannot scream lies at him daily".

[33]Heckscher, "Liberalism, fascism", 531, 540.

When the Swedish Economic Society debated the "milling obligation", Heckscher continued his campaign, saying

> that from the economic standpoint the measures which have been taken are worse than Russian economic planning inasmuch as they [the Russians] do know what they want and have adapted themselves to their goal accordingly. I shall not express an opinion as to whether what they want there makes any sense. However, to pursue economic planning without a plan, that is to say without a goal, is just a little too absurd.[34]

In early 1931, Wigforss published a lengthy review of a book about the Soviet five-year plan, written by one of the originators of the plan, who represented "the victorious Stalinist line of action".[35] Wigforss reproduced lots of "facts" from the book and assumed that eventually it would be possible to "penetrate the fog of propaganda and fantasies". Since the men behind the plan now hoped to fulfil it within four years, Wigforss assumed that the plan actually advanced according to plan: "It seems unlikely that such hopes would have been able to spread and take root if not the leading squad had been convinced that on the whole the original plan will be realized".[36]

Myrdal used the term economic planning in an article, contrasting "Planwirtschaft" to *laissez-faire*.[37] Otto Steiger, in his 1971 dissertation on the "new economics" in Sweden, claims that this was the first time Myrdal used the term. Curiously enough, he even claims that Myrdal was the first one to throw this concept into the debate.[38] Myrdal used the term again in the autumn, when he in a discussion with Heckscher

---

[34]Nationalekonomiska Föreningen, "Inmalningen och vår spannmålspolitik", March 23, 1931, 51. When government support for agriculture was discussed in the Economic Society several years later, Gustaf Åkerman referred back to Heckscher's opinions and stated that government is insensitive to risk and tardy in its economic affairs – it shows "a grave lack of calm adaption and flexibility". See Nationalekonomiska Föreningen, "Statsstödet åt jordbruket", February 28, 1935, 30.

[35]The author was G. Grinko and the title of the book was *Der Fünfjahrplan der UdSSR*.

[36]E. Wigforss, "Ryska femårsplanen", *Tiden* 23(1) (1931): 18, 26.

[37]G. Myrdal, "Kring den praktiska nationalekonomiens problematik", *Ekonomisk Tidskrift* 33(2) (1931): 60.

[38]O. Steiger, *Studien zur Entstehung der Neuen Wirtschaftslehre in Schweden: Eine Anti-Kritik* (Berlin: Duncker & Humblot, 1971).

in the Economic Society said that unemployment seemed hard to conquer unless one could "implement a more complete planned economy, which under Swedish conditions would imply vast industrial democracy".[39] Erik Lundberg believes that this was the first time the term planned economy was used in the Society,[40] but as we have seen, Heckscher used it already in the spring of 1931.

As the economic crisis deepened, accompanied by mounting criticism of capitalism, Cassel launched an aggressive counter-offensive. Socialists did not bother to analyse the causes of the crisis. "It is much easier to write a manifesto, which promises a perfect society, if you first of all can make a clean sweep with the old one". In reality, governments had caused the crisis through excessive nationalism, tariffs, subsidies, taxes and deflationary policies. The normal price formation process, the core of a capitalist society, had been brushed aside. "What are all these arbitrary interventions, other than examples of an unwillingness to recognize free price formation as the natural and very best regulator of production and distribution?"[41] In an editorial aimed against the idea of general over-production, Cassel drew the (for him) only possible conclusion: "If our economy could only be regulated by natural price formation based on a fixed monetary value, its capitalist character would constrain neither reasonable adaption of production according to needs, nor vigorous economic growth".[42] In yet another article, aimed at "dogmatic" socialists, Cassel repeated his diagnosis of the origins of the crisis:

Free market economy has not been allowed to develop according to its own laws but has been exposed to rough force, firstly through the war and the all but reasonable peace treaties and then by state intervention, which has on crucial points upset the conditions for a normal development of free enterprise. As "the capitalist order" has not been allowed to operate according to its own nature, it is obviously impossible to blame it for the crisis in which we have now ended up.[43]

[39]Nationalekonomiska Föreningen. "Arbetslösheten och dess behandling", October 12, 1931, 108.

[40]E. Lundberg, *Kriserna och ekonomerna* (Malmö: LiberFörlag, 1984).

[41]G. Cassel, "Kapitalistsamhället", *Svenska Dagbladet*, May 3, 1931.

[42]G. Cassel, "Överproduktion", *Svenska Dagbladet*, June 17, 1931.

[43]G. Cassel, "Understödspolitikens kris", *Svenska Dagbladet*, August 19, 1931.

Johan Åkerman in a book on economic progress and crises contrasted the real time-determined economy to the hypothetical timeless equilibrium economy. In this book, he concluded that business cycles and crises were not caused by organizational modes but by capital formation and stated the following:

> Even in a purely centralized, collectivistic community it is not possible to determine omnisciently how development will appear in five or ten years' time. It is not possible to foretell what inventions will be made in this or that industry, nor is it known what direction consumption will take. Should it go to the length of forbidding an industry to make use of an invention lest its productivity should exceed the programme of work, and regulate consumption in the most minute details without reference to the consumers, then plan economics will have triumphed. But then presumably it will have triumphed at the expense of progress.[44]

In a booklet on the world depression, Åkerman devoted some attention to the Russian five-year plan, with its "coercive measures to keep consumption low" and its focus on capital-creating industries. He concluded that "in a community in which money and credit do not form the basis of the entire productive life, drastic regulations have to be drawn up in order to give an impulse to the process of industrialization".[45] In a lecture at the Finnish Economic Society in October 1931, he questioned whether the Russian five-year plan, with its rapid capital formation, could achieve strong economic growth without running into crises:

> The planned economy believes it can escape the crisis by replacing the psychologically conditioned entrepreneurial activity in a capitalist society with a centralized working plan for increased capital formation in a communist state. However, it has forgotten the technological fact that production of means of production takes a long time, and that during this time changes must occur in production and consumption conditions. Even if you let the consumer, i.e. the present standard of living, pay for all these disturbances

---

[44]J. Åkerman, *Ekonomiskt framåtskridande och ekonomiska kriser* (Stockholm: Kooperativa Förbundets Bokförlag, 1931), 218. The book was published in English the following year: J. Åkerman, *Economic Progress and Economic Crises* (London: Macmillan, 1932), 170–171.

[45]J. Åkerman, *Some Lessons of the World Depression* (Stockholm: Nordiska Bokhandeln, 1931), 16.

related to progress, there will probably anyway be a general crisis, when the new means of production mature in large quantities.[46]

Gösta Bagge may have been a strong adversary of economic planning, but within his own field of expertise, his attitude was different. He had argued against planlessness within social policy in the 1920s. In 1929, he had joined a government committee assigned to work out a master plan for Swedish social policy and in March 1932, he spoke in Swedish radio on "The need for planning within social policy".[47]

A Very Undetermined Thing

As mentioned in the introduction, Leif Lewin tells us that it was Wigforss, who, during the socialization debate at the Social Democratic congress in March 1932, loosened the ties between socialization and planning. The economic planning ideology, with its goal of "a more general control over economic life", superseded the socialization ideology. The new ideology, like its predecessor, was vague in its contours. Lewin characterizes it as "a desire to strengthen the position of the state in economic life". But no particular method was specified for enlargement of the state nor was the scope of state activity indicated. "All that exists is a belief that it will become possible to satisfy the hunger for freedom of the multitude if the economic influence of the state is increased".[48] Wigforss himself has testified that a more pragmatic view of the means did not in any sense imply that the socialist end had been lost sight of: "Neither from the one side nor the other in the struggle has it been possible to see any obvious boundary to this socializing tendency of the planned economy, and on both contending fronts it has been possible to view every new step either as a battle won or a battle lost".[49]

---

[46]J. Åkerman, "Planhushållning och tidshushållning", *Ekonomiska Samfundets Tidskrift* 24 (1932): 6.

[47]Andreen, *Gösta Bagge som samhällsbyggare.*

[48]L. Lewin, *Planhushållningsdebatten* (Stockholm: Almqvist & Wiksell, 1967), 74–75, 78.

[49]Wigforss, "Ideologiska linjer", 530.

Wigforss published a review of Arthur Salter's book *Recovery* in May 1932. Salter's ambition was to combine competition and free enterprise with planning and his emphasis on free enterprise demonstrated "how deep his roots are anchored in the 19th century liberalism he denotes as outdated". Wigforss concluded that "the policy advocated has too many traits, which will scare away the usual supporters of capitalist recovery, but is not alien to the socialist movement, which builds upon the prospect of realizing a collectivist organization of the world economic life step by step".[50]

When Ohlin reviewed Salter's book, he did not appear as an impatient planner. He saw the book as "a masterly configuration of a program for liberalism's retreat to stronger positions, where one deems it possible to fight off attacks from the champions of 'economic planning'". Some types of economic planning, e.g. the state socialism that the Social Democrats had propagated before the war, would rather strengthen the economic causes for national antagonisms. As long as nationalism dominated the world, there was no prospect of economically efficient systems. "The attempt to portray the world economic crisis as the bankruptcy of the capitalist system, when in reality it is the bankruptcy of war and nationalism, must therefore be designated as abortive". However, the tendency was towards more of organization and intervention in economic life.[51] Ohlin also reviewed a book by Salter, Keynes and others on how to escape from the world crisis. In the book, Sir Basil Blackett advocated economic planning. Ohlin's comment was that one should perhaps not imitate Italy and Germany, but see "what one can learn from them" and he quoted Blackett's invitation to "think adventurously".[52]

Myrdal's emergence as an advocate for economic planning took place at the very end of an article on social policy in the short-lived journal *Spektrum*. Myrdal wrote the following:

---

[50]E. Wigforss, "Pånyttfödd kapitalism?" *Tiden* 24(5) (1932): 272.

[51]B. Ohlin, "Kris och planhushållning", *Stockholms-Tidningen*, July 12, 1932. Two years later, Salter's book *The Framework of an Ordered Society* was translated into Swedish. See A. Salter, *Planhushållning* (Stockholm: Tiden, 1934).

[52]B. Ohlin, "Hur krisen botas", *Stockholms-Tidningen*, August 7, 1932. The book reviewed was the Swedish translation of A. Salter, J. Stamp, J. M. Keynes, B. Blackett, H. Clay, and W. H. Beveridge, *The World's Economic Crisis and the Way of Escape* (London: George Allen and Unwin, 1931).

The idea which creeps in everywhere is that of *economic planning*. Corporate leaders and probably eventually their political allies are thinking along those lines. This idea is not alien to the labour movement; as a matter of fact it represents the content of the more radical socialism, after it let go the pure Marxist necessity dogma and thereby the attitude which assumed everything was finished after the revolution. Economic planning is a very undetermined thing, which leaves open for what purpose and interests planning is supposed to take place. [...] Economic planning means that one is prepared to go far enough with the measures so that they have maximum efficiency [...].[53]

In mid-September 1932, elections were held to the second chamber of the *Riksdag*. Karin Kock was a candidate for the Liberal Party. In a speech titled "Unemployment and economic policy", she argued for "a planned policy, which does not curtail political freedom and does not inhibit individual initiative".[54] The Liberal Party did not win any new seats but the Social Democrats won 14.

In late 1932, an extensive discussion on public works in times of depression unfolded in the Economic Society. Erik Lindahl gave an introduction whereupon a barrage of arguments ensued. On the one side was Bagge, Heckscher and Johan Åkerman; on the other side Lindahl and Ohlin. The basic issue was whether a new kind of works at market wages were to replace the old relief works at lower wages. The old works were self-liquidating since workers left them as soon as they could find work on free market terms. Bagge and Heckscher focused on the argument that public works at market wages would not be automatically self-liquidating in good times. They feared that these works would mushroom, resulting in an expansion of the public sector in the long run. In Heckscher's words:

All the probabilities suggest that if we embark upon public works which are to be liquidated by a decision to be taken at the beginning of the boom, people will deny that the boom has come. They will demand that

---

[53]G. Myrdal, "Socialpolitikens dilemma II", *Spektrum* 2(4) (1932): 30.
[54]Stockholms-Tidningen, "Liberal valstart i Bromma i går", *Stockholms-Tidningen*, September 7, 1932.

it should be regarded as a slump for as long as any difficulties are present in the economy, and there are always difficulties in the economy. [...] One does not need any deeper insight into socio-psychological factors to claim that the moment when people find the need for government interventions fulfilled, this moment will never come.[55]

Heckscher and Bagge therefore demanded institutional guarantees that the works be cancelled in boom periods, e.g. when unemployment fell to a previously defined level. Ohlin objected that it was conceivable that even members of parliament were able to learn something. Lindahl also figured that it would be possible to "replace this automatism with planned regulation". "I think it would be really bad if political life should malfunction in a way that one could not agree on an increase [of public works] which is not allowed to be permanent".[56]

Heckscher was the one connecting the planning of these works to the general issue of economic planning and he once more took as his point of departure the Russian five-year plans: "If it has been difficult to realize this plan, with time as the only limit, it will of course be much more difficult to realize a plan which is to be adapted to a curve of which one knows nothing".[57] This statement made Ohlin hit the ceiling:

Professor Heckscher thus really means that the Russian five-year plan, this violent transformation of the whole Russian economy in this enormous country, with changes of preconditions of production and transport and everything else, is a plan, which in no other essential respect is much more difficult to implement compared to public works in Sweden at 50 or 100 million kronor![58]

---

[55]Nationalekonomiska Föreningen, "Offentliga arbeten i depressionstider", November 25, 1932, 155–156.

[56]Ibid., 163.

[57]Ibid., 155. Some years later, Lindahl suggested a solution of the "timing" issue: All public works, where one could freely decide about timing, should be dependent upon two decisions: firstly, a decision about the appropriation within the yearly budget frame, and secondly, a later decision on when to start the works. He assumed that this solution would avoid the criticisms previously directed towards public works and would be in agreement with "the long-time planning within the public economy sector which is advocated in different quarters". See E. Lindahl, "Arbetslöshet och finanspolitik", *Ekonomisk Tidskrift* 37(1–2) (1935): 30.

[58]Nationalekonomiska Föreningen, "Offentliga arbeten", 161.

Increased government intervention, Ohlin argued, necessitated an inventory and rationalization of economic statistics. "Planning requires knowledge".[59] And statistics were forthcoming. In early 1933, a government report on the need for statistics on housing was published. The authors, Gunnar Myrdal and architect Uno Åhrén, argued for an investigation into housing "which could serve as *the necessary information basis for a long-term planned housing policy*". The contemporary housing market was described as "chaotic and anarchic". The solution of the housing problem required that "society"—state and municipalities—intervene and regulate "*with the purpose of leading and directing production as well as consumption of housing in a planned manner*".[60] Furthermore, an investigation into business cycles and public sector economy by Myrdal was published as an annex to the 1933 budget proposal; it was almost immediately published as a booklet. Myrdal discussed business cycle policy and social policy in general and public works in particular, but not, in any explicit way at least, economic planning.[61]

Dictatorship and Mismanagement

In an article on "Dictatorship and Technology", Heckscher outlined some of the ideas which were to mature in his lectures and articles on economic planning in subsequent years. Against a backdrop of events in the Soviet Union, Italy and Germany, he drew attention to the strengthened state power achieved by means of organization, large units, and control over the mails, telegraphs, stock exchanges, and (with Goebbels in mind) mass media such as newspapers, radio and movies. During the nineteenth century, the individual had been set free to transform technology and economy. Now these products were mobilized against the freedom that had given them birth. "And the tool is the new state",

---

[59]B. Ohlin, "Planmässighetens krav", *Stockholms-Tidningen*, December 18, 1932.

[60]*Undersökning rörande behovet av en utvidgning av bostadsstatistiken jämte vissa därmed förbundna bostadspolitiska frågor* (Stockholm: Isaac Marcus Boktryckeri-Aktiebolag, 1933) (SOU 1933: 14), 89, 91–92.

[61]G. Myrdal, *Konjunktur och offentlig hushållning: En utredning* (Stockholm: Kooperativa förbundets bokförlag, 1933).

wrote Heckscher, and found it "irrefutable that all 'economic planning', however implemented, leads to a loss of the individual's intellectual and spiritual freedom". The only way out was to use the governmental tool to defend the foundations laid in the nineteenth century. "To begin with, it means protecting one's own country against Bolshevik-Fascist-Nazi tendencies".[62]

A week later, Heckscher urged his fellow countrymen to defend the Swedish rule of law against Nazis and Communists. In this connection, he asked how anybody could dream of economic planning without regulation of wages. One of the main pillars of Soviet Russian planning was that workers' wages and organizations were controlled from above. "Thus, those in power in Russia are far more consistent than Western planning supporters".[63]

At this point, in the midst of the depression, Cassel again attacked the ideas that general overproduction could occur and that governments could handle capital investments better than capitalists. Economic progress had over the long run been smooth and its pace determined by the supply of capital.

> The talk, now so commonly heard, of the need to replace the planlessness of private capital investment with "economic planning" by the state is in any case not supported by any experience demonstrating that the state can make a better job of it. What has brought the world economy into an unprecedented depression, which threatens to end up in a total breakdown, is without any doubt partly the mismanagement of the functions which belong to the states, partly increasing state interventions in other areas.[64]

Cassel cited as examples of the first kind mismanagement of the monetary system and protectionism, as examples of the second kind recent malinvestments in Britain, Brazil and the US. He ended with a fusillade: "The idea that the state as a higher being would raise the national economy from the swamp, where 'capitalism' has allowed it to end up,

---

[62]E. Heckscher, "Diktatur och teknik", *Dagens Nyheter*, March 22, 1933.
[63]E. Heckscher, "Försvaret mot omstörtningen", *Dagens Nyheter*, March 29, 1933.
[64]G. Cassel, "Överproduktion, planhushållning", *Svenska Dagbladet*, April 2, 1933.

seems to be a hypocrisy intended to throw a veil over the states' real responsibility for the crisis".

Cassel completely dismissed the idea that there were unused savings. Consequently, the government could not create new employment through public works but would only crowd out existing employment. Any public measures to counteract unemployment must be funded through an increased money supply by the central bank. There was thus a need for swift action according to a plan where government, parliament, central bank and trade unions coordinated their actions. But this had not happened.[65]

Ohlin on his part wholeheartedly supported Keynes' recipe for recovery—increased liquidity and increased public demand through public works—and pointed to the multiplier effect: "When you hire two workers, at least one worker will thereby be employed in the private sector, and unemployment benefits for three are saved".[66]

When the new unemployment policy was discussed in the Economic Society in April 1933, Heckscher in his introduction could not refrain from a short reference to the planning issue. Economic planning of any kind must take into consideration the most important cost element: wages. "The advocates of economic planning therefore have special reason to pay attention to the wage level, and leaders of the Soviet economy would surely laugh if someone told them, that they could pursue their economic planning on the basis of wages not decided in accordance with their demands".[67]

Ohlin insisted that new circumstances require new solutions, not least for a liberal:

The central theme in the post-war liberal social outlook is not 19th century "laissez faire". Otherwise all social policy must be rejected. In reality neither this, nor the undertaking of more planning in economic life, are in conflict with a generally liberal attitude. The practical consequences vary according

---

[65]G. Cassel, "Bristande planhushållning", *Svenska Dagbladet*, April 7, 1933.

[66]B. Ohlin, "Väg ur depressionen: Keynes får instämmande från Times", *Stockholms-Tidningen*, April 2, 1933.

[67]Nationalekonomiska Föreningen, "Arbetslöshetspolitiken", April 28, 1933, 85.

to times and circumstances. Nothing is so alien to its [liberalism's] essence as a sterile clinging to a past epoch which time has outgrown.[68]

On May 27, 1933, an agreement on crisis policy was reached between the Social Democrats and the Agrarian Party; the measures to be taken would cost 180 million *kronor*, of which 100 million were allocated to public works. This was the so-called cow trade (*kohandeln*). We cannot account for the following extensive discussion of public works since it would take us too far from the planning theme. However, there was, of course, as we have already seen, a connection between crisis policy based on public works and economic planning. A market liberal like Heckscher was acutely aware of this connection, as evidenced by his posts in the debate in the Economic Society six months earlier.

Roosevelt Makes His Entrance

During the summer of 1933, Ohlin devoted a series of articles to Franklin Roosevelt's New Deal; half a dozen articles had the latter's name in the headline. Ohlin concluded that Roosevelt had been granted dictatorial authority from Congress on all issues. "His ability to charm Americans can only be compared with Hitler's influence over the German people".[69] Ohlin discussed public works, the issuing of new bank notes and the limitation of agricultural production, and he disassociated himself from the underconsumption theory which was behind the attempts to raise wages in order to increase purchasing power. Ohlin assessed Roosevelt's overarching ambition in the following way:

You would completely misunderstand his intentions if you believe that he would leave prewar capitalism free rein after he has pulled it out of the ditch and had it passably repaired. Far from that! The plan is to create a

---

[68]B. Ohlin, "Den fria världsmarknaden", *Stockholms-Tidningen*, May 16, 1933.
[69]B. Ohlin, "Roosevelts ekonomiska politik", *Stockholms-Tidningen*, June 2, 1933.

social-capitalist order as far from Manchester liberal prewar capitalism as possible.[70]

The alternative to Roosevelt would have been a more revolutionary system with communist features. The question, according to Ohlin, was whether Roosevelt's dictatorial powers would be temporary or permanent. He mapped Roosevelt's "brain trust" and gave the following verdict: "Intellectual lawyers and economists, who combine social reform zeal and a belief in the necessity of planning with an obvious skepticism towards economic authorities of the old school".[71]

Ohlin expressed his surprise that in these revolutionary times—with communism in Russia, fascism in Italy, Nazism in Germany, Rooseveltism in the US—there still remained people in the quiet Nordic corner of the world who were "horrified by every step in the economic policy of their own country which deviates from the old usual". He apparently had his old teachers in mind when he referred to "the recognized authorities [who are] tethered by prewar experiences". "The key word is organization", exclaimed Ohlin and concluded that this, in the near future, meant that states "see to their immediate interests and organize accordingly".[72]

The liberal era, Ohlin proclaimed, in an editorial titled "Organization and adaptation", was an exception in the evolution of human society:

> Economic history shows that the social organization adapts to technological, sociological and psychological conditions and that this adaption only in exceptional cases entails a Manchester liberal type of society. Consider guilds, trade monopolies and all other social institutions which for centuries have made up the foundation for economic life! Against an historical backdrop, the latter part of the 19th century with its "laisser faire"

---

[70]B. Ohlin, "Amerikas experiment: Det är med prisstegring som med vin: verkan beror på kvantiteten", *Stockholms-Tidningen*, July 20, 1933. Ohlin later elaborated on Roosevelt and the underconsumption theory: B. Ohlin, "Roosevelts prövotid", *Stockholms-Tidningen*, August 20, 1933.

[71]B. Ohlin, "Ordnad revolution hellre än kommunistisk! Männen kring Amerikas nye president", *Stockholms-Tidningen*, July 30, 1933.

[72]B. Ohlin, "Den revolutionära verkligheten", *Stockholms-Tidningen*, August 5, 1933.

imprint stands out as a short transition period conditioned by certain technological changes.[73]

Now, these changes had taken a new direction with large-scale production, monopolies, business cycles, agricultural overproduction. You might wish away some of these tendencies, but to what avail? "From the perspective of a single country the condition in other countries must be seen as given and economic policy be adjusted accordingly. That policies under these conditions must be *opportunistic* is obvious". Economic policy could not be fixed according to state socialist or old liberal ideas but always had to be adapted to new conditions. The main task was to "create opportunities for more production and distribution according to plan without suffocating private initiative through bureaucratic centralization". Planning initiatives could concern investments and location of industries. "One must create an elastic frame, within which private initiatives and associations can shape a reasonably planned development". This would require politicians to know more about economic and social conditions than hitherto. This, in turn, meant that they must have access to better economic statistics and knowledge about social trends. This would not be as difficult to achieve in a small country like Sweden, with a population on a high cultural level and a government pursuing a "non-doctrinaire" economic policy, as in the larger countries.[74]

When a strike among construction workers threatened the Swedish government's public works programme, Ohlin cautioned that economic planning would be rendered impossible if independent groups of citizens did not take public interest into reasonable consideration.[75]

Cassel's first evaluation of "Roosevelt's experiment" appeared in the late summer of 1933. Regulation of the monetary supply was a basic government responsibility and the drastic US deflation over several years had to be counteracted by an increased monetary supply to

---

[73]B. Ohlin, "Organisation och anpassning", *Stockholms-Tidningen*, August 13, 1933. Wennås notes that adaptation and organization were key words in Ohlin's vocabulary. See O. Wennås, "Bertil Ohlin om socialismen, liberalismen och folkpartiet", in *Liberal ideologi och politik 1934–1984* (Falköping: AB Folk & samhälle, 1984).

[74]B. Ohlin, "Organisation och anpassning".

[75]B. Ohlin, "Byggnadskonflikten", *Stockholms-Tidningen*, August 22, 1933.

raise the general price level. Instead of taking this course of action, Roosevelt had "undertaken the most violent interventions in the national economy". "Such crude measures as are now applied in the United States cannot be expected to result in any real equilibrium in the national economy, and thus the American experiment will surely fail". Roosevelt's actions were based on "a number of delusions, often of a very amateurish kind", such as the idea that consumption could not keep pace with production and that entrepreneurial profit was the villain of the piece. Cassel declared that "there can never exist any purchasing power other than the one originating from production itself" (i.e. he swore allegiance to Say's law). But Roosevelt seemed to "have very little respect for economic theory" at the same time as he indulged in economic theories, primarily "in those conveyed by pure dilettanti".[76]

Already in the 1920s, Cassel had raged against "superstitious" faith in state action, management and control, and in a "Christmas discourse" of 1933 he coupled this confession of faith with the new "catchword": "Since the war, the belief in the absolute rationality and effectiveness of state management of trade and industry has found its principal expression in a catchword which seems to exercise an almost hypnotic effect on the mass of people. This catchword is 'economic planning'".[77] Cassel assumed that the term originated from Russia, where it was characterized by forced savings and capital construction, thus by an ambition to make the economy more "capitalist", at the same time as people in the West complained about exaggerated capital formation and neglect of consumption. Cassel also repeated his demand for "economic planning" in management of the monetary system. "But when this is called for, the reply from governments and central banks is that it is impossible and that they cannot accept responsibility for maintaining a stable monetary system".[78] Cassel furthermore reacted against the confusion of state and society. "The state is not at all identic with society, and very important societal interests are actually met by private industry without state participation".[79]

---

[76]G. Cassel, "Roosevelts Experiment", *Svenska Dagbladet*, August 23, 1933.
[77]G. Cassel, "Staten och näringslivet", *Sunt Förnuft* 13(December) (1933): 399.
[78]Ibid.
[79]Ibid., 397.

In another Christmas discourse, Cassel took Roosevelt's industrial codes and agricultural cuts as examples of planning failures. One intervention must lead to another in a never-ending sequence: "All things in economic life are intimately interconnected with thousands of threads, so that one intervention here directly necessitates an intervention there, and one is therefore forced to continue almost infinitely without being able to restore any equilibrium".[80] Cassel's last words that year were blistering: "Dictatorships and 'planned economy'" with "gross delusions and dilettante quackery" competed for influence over political leaders.[81]

Ohlin also had something to say about economy and democracy. He had been provoked by an article claiming that a democratic state is not well suited to handle economic issues and should therefore limit itself to uphold the rule of law.[82] Ohlin admitted that democracy has many weaknesses: Antagonisms between interest groups are sometimes so fierce that government loses its ability to take action. Politicians and officials are not selected according to their ability to solve economic problems. Political parties have to "appeal to the large and economically partially ignorant mass of citizens". However, a government exclusively concerned with the rule of law would be an atavism in an era when technological and economic developments fostered natural monopolies and large-scale production. The way forward had to go through economic education of the citizens. Even so, many problems were so complicated that they could only be solved by experts. The mass of the people must therefore have enough sense to understand when problems should be left to "those qualified".[83]

The Debate Takes Off

The economic planning debate took off in earnest at the beginning of 1934. In Lewin's words:

---

[80]G. Cassel, "Roosevelt som reformator", *Svenska Dagbladet*, December 23, 1933.
[81]G. Cassel, "Meningslös förödelse", *Svenska Dagbladet*, December 31, 1933.
[82]Sunt Förnuft, "Ekonomi och demokrati", *Sunt Förnuft* 13(9) (1933).
[83]B. Ohlin, "Ekonomi och demokrati", *Stockholms-Tidningen*, December 30, 1933.

When the economic recovery arrived at last and the Social Democrats – as expected – declared that they would now continue to increase the influence of the state over economic life, every vestige of uncertainty was dispelled [...]. One issue of domestic policy dominated all others, and the economic planning debate, on rigid ideological lines, got under way. The authoritative indication of the long-term economic intentions of the Social Democrats was given in the 1934 budget and finance bill.[84]

The Conservatives, the Liberal Party and various business organizations set about organizing a defence campaign. Common arguments, says Lewin in his account of the debate, were that economic planners suffer from blind faith in the state, that state administration is bureaucratic and ineffective in itself, that politicians are unfit for economic tasks, that nobody is capable of central management of the economy, that economic planning leads to a rigid economy, that the increase of prosperity enjoyed since the nineteenth century could never have taken place under a planned economy, and that one control will lead to another in a vicious circle. Particularly pregnant, according to Lewin, was the right-wing argument touching on the risks to foreign trade and the value of the currency. But the possibly most important argument concerned the link between economic and personal freedom.

Myrdal opened the year with a report on the effects of fiscal policy, an extensive (280 pages) annex to the report of the unemployment committee which had been working since 1927.[85] The report was presented in one of the major daily newspapers as a "program for detailed implementation of economic planning".[86] However, this characteristic seems somewhat exaggerated. Myrdal's own characteristic seems more to the point: "A rather circumstantial theoretical apparatus with alternative, often very unrealistic preconditions of a methodological kind

---

[84]Lewin, *Planhushållningsdebatten*, 98.

[85]For an overview of the activities of the committee, see E. Wadensjö, "The Committee on Unemployment and the Stockholm School", in *The Stockholm School of Economics Revisited*, ed. L. Jonung (Cambridge: Cambridge University Press, 1991).

[86]A. Lgr., "Ekonomisk veckorevy", *Dagens Nyheter*, January 14, 1934.

[…]."[87] Anyway, Myrdal in his introduction made some remarks aimed at economic planning. He concluded that "pure" market price formation had never existed and was in reality unthinkable. Price formation is always conditioned by regulations imposed by society. Consequently, *"one can of course set as a goal to change the course of price formation as one wishes through a planned arrangement of this institutional frame"*.[88] There were fairly fixed regulations, the laws and norms which regulate property rights and contractual arrangements, and there were flexible regulations in the shape of fiscal, monetary, credit, trade and social policies. Myrdal in his report took aim at the latter type, in particular at the fiscal regulations. In one section of the report, where he wrote about public works, he raised the issue of long-term planning. If the use of fiscal policy as a counter-cyclical instrument were to be effective, improvisations would not suffice, but long-term planning would be required:

> Long-term planning does not mean, as someone once incorrectly stated, to lock expenditure into an inflexible scheme. On the contrary, it is a necessary precondition for a rational adaptation to changing circumstances. [---] Extended and improved long-term planning is probably the field where the most important and profound fiscal reforms will take place.[89]

Kock opened the first Economic Society meeting of 1934 with a presentation of Roosevelt's reconstruction policy. She characterized Roosevelt's long-term ambitions as "an attempt to create a planned economy founded on an individual basis" but refrained from further comments on planning and instead stuck to business cycle related issues.[90] However, at the next

---

[87]G. Myrdal, *Finanspolitikens ekonomiska verkningar.* Annex 5 to Arbetslöshetsutredningens betänkande II (Stockholm: Kungl. Boktryckeriet/P. A. Norstedt & Söner, 1934) (SOU 1934:1), 6.

[88]Ibid., 3. Myrdal uses the terms regulations and institutions interchangeably.

[89]Ibid., 140–141.

[90]Nationalekonomiska Föreningen, "Roosevelts rekonstruktionsprogram ur konjunktursynpunkt", January 22, 1934, 2. The presentation was soon published in a somewhat extended version: K. Kock, *Roosevelts program ur konjunktursynpunkt* (Stockholm: Kooperativa förbundets bokförlag, 1934). The book got many positive reviews in newspapers and journals. As Brisman wrote: "The author has wisely been careful about making judgements; the publication mainly has the character of a purely factual account […]. See S. Brisman, "Ekonomiska småskrifter", *Göteborgs Handels- och Sjöfartstidning*, April 24, 1934.

meeting of the society – in spite of running the risk of being associated with "theoreticians of Nazi colour"—she pointed to long-term unemployment as a problem "which demands certain planned economy".[91]

Cassel once more underlined that economic planning has a "strong cumulative effect", where one intervention causes another, and that one would have to be blind not to see that it leads to economic dictatorship and then to general dictatorship, irrespective of whether the underlying ideology expresses itself in terms of Bolshevism, fascism, Nazism or Roosevelt policy.[92]

Myrdal Versus Cassel

On 1 March 1934, Myrdal succeeded Cassel as professor of economics at Stockholm University.[93] His inaugural lecture was a passionate plea for economic planning. He explained that this idea had deep historical roots both to the left and to the right of the political spectrum. Rejection of the liberal idea of harmony of interest was the common denominator behind the demands for planning:

> In contrast, planning efforts in their variety of all kinds originate from the necessity of centralized economic management. You don't trust private initiative, individual responsibility and the free play of economic forces. You demand deeper interventions. These interventions target the very "system", production and exchange, money and credit, i.e. the sections of price formation which liberalism as a matter of principle wished to defend from interventions. [---] Demands for planning – emanating from both right and left – [...] have always required a dynamic view of society and its institutions whereby the liberal static

---

[91]Nationalekonomiska Föreningen, "Aktuell arbetslöshet och arbetslöshetspolitik", April 27, 1934, 114.

[92]G. Cassel, "Planhushållning och diktatur", *Svenska Dagbladet*, February 25, 1934.

[93]Dagens Nyheter, "Gunnar Myrdal intog sin post med idéprogram", *Dagens Nyheter*, March 2, 1934. Cassel had already in a letter of March 8, 1930, told Myrdal that he (Myrdal) must be available to succeed him (Cassel) when he retired. Myrdal replied in a letter of March 24 that this was "the professorship in the whole world, I would prefer to work within".

societal abstraction under "the system" has been broken into pieces and relativized.[94]

According to Myrdal, the increasing volume of state interventions did not emanate from any quest for planning. On the contrary, the increasing volume of interventions required planning. He also dismissed the idea that increased state intervention threatened "freedom" with a strange formula which seems aimed directly at his predecessor: "The perception that economic 'freedom' and 'compulsion' respectively, in general, in society as a whole, can be greater or lesser, is a metaphysic apriorism of the very type which distinguishes the methodologically naïve market liberalism".[95]

Myrdal explained how conditions in contemporary society differed from the old liberal society. The liberal society had been distinguished by a frame of stable institutions (habits, attitudes) within which small and mobile economic units enacted their competitive struggle. Over time, the framework had become less stable and economic units had become bigger, more powerful and less mobile; they could now themselves design the rules of the game. In this situation, "the government *must* intervene to prevent chaos and breakdown". Myrdal furthermore argued that planning during WWI had opened up "undreamt-of opportunities", in contrast to the many pundits who had dismissed it as a failure. There was also a need for "a kind of international economic planning" between central banks regarding business cycles and monetary matters. Myrdal noted that his predecessor Cassel had pursued a heroic but futile struggle on this frontier.[96]

In order to kill the remaining doubts of his audience, Myrdal portrayed economic planning as fated: It was not an alternative which could be chosen or not chosen. It was a necessity. The government had been forced into economic life by prevailing conditions and could not withdraw since these conditions remained. This scenario gave Myrdal

---

[94]G. Myrdal, "Installationsföreläsning den 31 mars 1934", in *Samhällskrisen och socialvetenskaperna* (Stockholm: Kooperativa förbundets bokförlag, 1935), 19–20. The dating in the title ought to be March 1 and not March 31.

[95]Ibid., 23.

[96]Ibid., 28–29, 31.

the opportunity to deliver a final blow to his predecessor: "Market liberalism will not be a feasible policy but an outdated utopia nourished by occasional untimely social dreamers, an increasingly pale and idealized mirage from a lost golden age".[97]

Cassel's reply came quickly. He attacked the "delusions" of economic planning and once more took aim at the planners' recklessness before the issue of general economic equilibrium:

> The free economy solves this huge bookkeeping issue through price formation. Its task is to bring about the necessary equilibrium between supply of means of production and demand for final products. [...] There are always those who think that they have to pay too much for final products or that they receive too little for their productive efforts. However, free price formation enforces a reconciliation of these opposing views and causes all parties to make the concessions required to achieve economic equilibrium. After severe economic upheavals it is of course more difficult than usual to achieve such equilibrium. Demands are made for other prices than those admitted by the market, different interest groups try to push through higher or lower prices for different accomplishments by force. The economic need for price formation is pushed aside as a problematic obstacle. Of course the result is that price formation can no longer fulfil its task of creating equilibrium, and that the economy becomes more and more distorted. In this way the idea of economic planning evolves, which once for all is supposed to make everything right.[98]

The worst recklessness among planners had to do with their ideas about capital formation. They did not care about equilibrium in this area. They figured that there are always "capitalists" who can supply the necessary means. "That such expenses must be paid for by new savings is an economic truth which they have not yet discovered". Plans for economic planning were made with the intent to root out capitalism under the quiet presumption that private capital and capital formation still would be at the disposal of the state. Cassel pointed to the Russian

---

[97]Ibid., 37. In spite of these remarks, Cassel is supposed to have told Myrdal that he was the most dangerous man in the country, but that no one else was worthy of being his (Cassel's) successor.

[98]G. Cassel, "Planekonomiens villfarelser", *Svenska Dagbladet*, March 3, 1934.

example, where enormous demands for real capital had been handled through starvation of the people, and Roosevelt's "dictatorship", which attempted to raise the living standard of the people at the expense of capital formation. Communist Russia had thus gone astray in "capitalist" direction while capitalist America had brushed capital aside.

This post triggered a rejoinder by a Liberal member of the *Riksdag*, Oscar Carlström. He asked what would have happened with Swedish agriculture if the government had not intervened and himself gave the answer that "we would not have had any food production in this country". Such a blow to the agricultural population would probably have led to dictatorship. "If government is dumbfounded before such a situation, people will pass it by and fall into the arms of any subversive powers".[99] Cassel's reaction, in view of the dire counterfactual scenario presented by Carlström, was pretty defensive: "It is when we go farther in intervention, regulation and subsidy than what necessity demands, that we begin to call for – both nationally and internationally – a development towards economic planning and dictatorship".[100]

A couple of days later, Minister of Finance Wigforss talked about economic planning and used the word "people's community" (*folkgemenskap*). An editorial in *Svenska Dagbladet* drew parallels to the German *Volksgemeinschaft* and asked if this was going to replace Prime Minister Per Albin Hansson's People's Home. Wigforss' ideas were contrasted to those of Cassel. Conclusion: "Economic planning equals government economic dictatorship".[101]

Bagge and the Conservative Spirit

Bagge launched attacks on economic planning in two speeches in March 1934. In the first speech, he characterized the concept as "somewhat capricious and elusive" and figured planning had been added to

[99]O. Carlström, "Planhushållning och diktatur", *Svenska Dagbladet*, March 4, 1934.
[100]G. Cassel, "Professor Cassel preciserar sin uppfattning", *Svenska Dagbladet*, March 4, 1934.
[101]Svenska Dagbladet, "Klasskamp mot folkgemenskap", *Svenska Dagbladet*, March 7, 1934.

the Social Democratic Party programme to make "old socialist rem-
nants" more appetizing.[102] He referred to a statement by Prime Minister
Hansson in conjunction with the budget and finance bill, according to
which business cycle policy was to be succeeded by economic planning.
He furthermore, referring to a speech by Wigforss, assumed that this
planning would force business life to adapt to trade union demands.
However, in the nations from which the idea of planning had been borrowed, Russia, Germany and Italy, the right to work had been trans-
formed into an obligation to work under any conditions; there was
dictatorship also in the labour market.

In the second speech, titled "The Planned Economy", Bagge once
more complained about the ambiguity of the concept—"it is like the
chameleon which changes colour according to its background, sometimes red, sometimes black, sometimes quite mélange"—and homed in
on the economic planning proposals in the budget and finance bill.[103]
Clearly it was the public works at market wages which occasioned the
biggest apprehensions for the future. If economic life had to adapt to
meet trade union wage demands, the labour market would ossify, and
central and local authorities would be forced to maintain unprofitable
production, which would lead to socialist economic planning. Bagge
also held that government economic planning "is distinguished neither
by plan nor by economy", just as the Holy Roman Empire was neither
holy, Roman or empire, he characterized communist and Nazi experiments as "planless command economy", he cited the United States, where
policy exhibited planlessness "of grotesque dimensions", and Russia,
where capitalist economic fluctuations had been replaced by periodical
famines.[104] Out of deference to the conservative ideological heritage,
however, he also felt obligated to mark the boundary vis-a-vis liberalism
and dissociate himself from *laissez-faire* policy. In the end, therefore, the
crucial factor in appraising government interventions was the spirit in
which they were carried out: "Conservatism wishes to avoid both liberal

---

[102]G. Bagge, *Svensk konservatism och tidslägets krav: Fyra föredrag* (Södertälje: Axlings Bok- och Tidskriftstryckeri, 1934), 15.

[103]Ibid., 25.

[104]Ibid., 33, 36.

laissez-faire policy and overstrain of the public sector by tasks it cannot manage. Conservative policy above all wants to build upon experience and avoid unrealistic constructions of the current planning type".[105] As Aronson concludes: "The ultimate purpose of a measure is crucial [for Bagge], if it is to remedy a specific problem and strengthen the existing social order or if the measure is motivated with regard to a socialist ultimate objective".[106]

Modern dictatorships were born out of crises. But what would happen when economies recovered? Ohlin was pretty pessimistic. Opinions could be controlled on an unprecedented scale through newspapers and radio. "Stalin has noticed, Goebbels follows in his footsteps".[107]

Cassel on Planning Failures

In April, Cassel, in the presence of Prime Minister Hansson, delivered an address on "The Planned Economy" to the annual conference of the Federation of Swedish Industries (*Industriförbundet*), where he attributed economic planning ideas to "the ancient blind faith in a supreme leadership which represents the acme of reason", a blind faith cultivated ever since Plato's day by "speculative spirits" in their attempts to design ideal societies without reference to the complications entailed in change and progress. He went on to remind that Europe had experienced several hundred years of mercantilism, and he felt that planning enthusiasts "would do wisely to devote a few evening hours to a study of various chapters in the history of mercantilism". Liberalism's "bold idea", to the effect that coherent management of economic life was unnecessary, translated into action, had led to the mightiest economic leap forward of all time. But the generations which were now able to enjoy "the fruits

---

[105]Ibid., 37. Bagge's speeches got attention particularly in Conservative newspapers; see Svenska Dagbladet, "Regeringen har ingenting lärt, ingenting glömt", *Svenska Dagbladet*, March 7, 1934 and "Planhushållning ett fantasiens gyckelord", *Svenska Dagbladet*, March 28, 1934.

[106]T. Aronson, *Gösta Bagges politiska tänkande: En studie i 1900-talets svenska konservatism* (Stockholm: Norstedts Juridik, 1993), 153.

[107]B. Ohlin, "Diktaturernas uppkomst", *Stockholms-Tidningen*, April 4, 1934.

of more than a century of development of such brilliant character" had come to regard progress as a matter of course, and, after a few disturbances of the world economy, were ready "to throw the whole of this social order on the junk pile".[108]

> It is in this psychological situation that the idea of a "planned economy" found sustenance and grew to a dominant force in present-day opinion. The call for authoritative and rational management of society in our time is not by any means only raised in what are usually called revolutionary circles: it also has a strong influence in the bourgeois world. But the new current of opinion has been thought out in terms of neither economic history nor economic theory. "Economic planning" has simply become a fad, and people who want to be in the swim adopt ideas of economic planning about as uncritically as they take up other fashionable fancies, be it in clothes, life style, or opinion.[109]

Cassel tried to deprive the economic planners of this appeal of fashion, firstly by shifting responsibility for the crisis, secondly by citing instances of economic planning failures. In an attempt to turn the planners' weapons against themselves, he declared that it was governments, not private business and industry, which bore the guilt of the crisis. It was governments which had started war, demanded exorbitant reparations, resorted to protectionism, and conducted deflationary policies. Unhappy examples of economic planning could furthermore be experienced by anyone who cared to take a simple stroll in the sunshine: "No Stockholmer can have received any very strong impression of economic planning when he has walked around in the summertime and felt annoyed by the way the streets are incessantly being torn up and relaid for different purposes [...]."[110] Examples of unsuccessful economic planning on a larger scale were not lacking either. In the Soviet Union, huge industries were built but transportation and distribution

---

[108]G. Cassel, *"Planhushållning" Diskussion med inledningsföredrag av professor Gustav Cassel vid Sveriges Industriförbunds årsmöte den 17 April 1934* (Stockholm, 1934), 3–5.
[109]Ibid., 5.
[110]Ibid.

were overlooked. In the United States, farmers were paid large sums for sowing, while simultaneously they were paid equally large sums for destroying what they had cultivated. Rational economic planning evidently did not come about merely because some government body took over economic tasks.

> The advocates of economic planning have decided to sweep aside this objection by collecting all government bodies under a single hand, thus placing the entire social order under one dictatorial management. We see here how the idea of economic planning leads with inescapable logic to the idea of dictatorship.[111]

But not even dictatorship achieved any great successes, as was demonstrated by the violent changes of course undergone by Russian policy. Neither could it be any different:

> When all will is concentrated in one place, quite naturally the result will be that events are allowed to run too far in one direction before the leadership perceives the need to change course, and even farther before it succeeds in forming and implementing the measures required to do this. Back in a social order based on an infinity of individual initiatives, every development has to reckon with a natural reaction which puts a stop to it before it goes too far in one direction.[112]

Public authorities were acting too slowly to counteract crises and the desire to heap more responsibility upon them had overstrained the state so that it was beginning to "to suffer from symptoms which we are accustomed to find among neurasthenic persons".[113]

Cassel's speech triggered a lively debate among the industrial elite. At the following dinner, Per Albin Hansson successfully—if measured by the applause—poured oil on troubled waters: "My idea is that economic

---

[111]Ibid., 7.
[112]Ibid.
[113]Ibid., 8.

planning should be made not by politicians but by capable business-men, so that we can get the most out of the good forces".[114]

In May, Cassel delivered a "Richard Cobden Lecture" in London titled "From Protectionism through Planned Economy to Dictatorship". In step with the spread of protectionism, he declared, governments became more and more entangled in the affairs of private businesses and industry, which lent nourishment to the idea of a planned economy under the management of a central authority. However, this management would be confronted with more problems and complications than any planner could imagine in his wildest dreams. The consequence would be series after series of mistakes, all necessitating further interventions. Take the single example of the difficulties involved in achieving the right balance between saving and consumption. In the Soviet Union, capital investment was force-fed more than in any capitalist country, whereas the capitalist United States endeavoured to maintain consumption and neglected capital formation. Cassel drew the following conclusion:

> The leadership of the state in economic affairs which advocates of Planned Economy want to establish, is, as we have seen, necessarily connected with a bewildering mass of government interferences of a steadily cumulative nature. The arbitrariness, the mistakes and the inevitable contradictions of such policy will, as daily experience shows, only strengthen the demand for a more rational coordination of the different measures and, therefore, for unified leadership. For this reason Planned Economy will always tend to develop into Dictatorship.[115]

A parliament was no guarantee against this development. On the contrary, it could not fulfil all the duties which economic leadership

---

[114]Dagens Nyheter, "Planhushållning förkastas av industrin", *Dagens Nyheter*, April 18, 1934; Svenska Dagbladet, "'Kapitalismen har gjort underverk'. Prof. Cassel gisslar skarpt planhushållningssvärmeriet", *Svenska Dagbladet*, April 18, 1934.

[115]G. Cassel, "From Protectionism Through Planned Economy to Dictatorship", *International Conciliation*. Documents for the year 1934. New York (1934): 323. This quote and more from the Cobden Lecture appeared a decade later in the *New York Times*. It was displayed as an example of his "great wisdom and insight" and said to be "prophetic in the light of events since that time". See New York Times, "Gustav Cassel's Warning", *New York Times*, January 17, 1945.

required without being drawn into the struggle between different pressure groups and being corrupted. Moreover, the parliament would be continually overstrained through having to consider the infinity of complicated questions associated with the private sector. Conclusion: "The parliamentary system can be saved only by wise and deliberate restriction of the functions of parliaments".[116] Let dictatorship once be established in economic affairs and it would gradually penetrate into other areas and threaten fundamental values such as personal freedom, freedom of thought and expression, and the independence of science.

In his memoirs, Cassel recalls that his lecture aroused considerable interest in Britain and the US, where the Carnegie Endowment for International Peace spread the message to "leading men" and published it in its International Conciliation series.[117]

Ohlin, in turn, during the spring of 1934, argued that the economic recovery had gained so much momentum that it was time to reduce the number of loan-financed public works.[118] The most urgent task was to "create plan and order in the economic policy measures that had been hastily introduced during the crisis and adapt them to the long-term requirement". "One could talk about 'framework planning' rather than about a planned economy".[119] The concept of framework planning was further explained:

It is about creating a frame for economic life – and to adapt it according to changes in e.g. our relation to economic life in other countries – so that crisis tendencies can be counteracted and arrested in time. Within the given frame, free initiative can assert itself without burdening control. [...] Typical examples of measures of a "framework character" are tariff and monetary policies. Measures of this kind are aimed at keeping production running [...] without putting a strait-jacket on the business community.[120]

---

[116]Cassel, "From Protectionism", 324.

[117]G. Cassel, *I förnuftets tjänst*, vol. 2 (Stockholm: Natur och Kultur, 1941), 394.

[118]See, e.g., B. Ohlin, "Bör finanspolitiken omläggas?", *Stockholms-Tidningen*, April 26, 1934 and "Budgeten och framtiden", *Stockholms-Tidningen*, June 16, 1934.

[119]B. Ohlin, "En ny ekonomisk politik?", *Stockholms-Tidningen*, July 25, 1934.

[120]B. Ohlin, "Socialism och krispolitik", *Stockholms-Tidningen*, August 26, 1934.

Ohlin also came back to Roosevelt's policies. He noted the confusing mix of expansionary and contractionary measures.[121] Roosevelt had nonetheless demonstrated "that drive and energy and swift action is just as possible in democratic societies as in dictatorships".[122]

Frankenstein's Monster

In May, Myrdal, Kock and Heckscher participated in a radio debate about economic policy. Kock gave an overview of the theme. Myrdal appeared pessimistic about the economic situation and stressed the need for further state intervention in agriculture, industry and foreign trade. Heckscher dismissed the whole idea of economic planning as a myth and pointed to the United States: "It is hard to find anything which is farther from economic planning in any sensible way".[123]

In an article on "Planned Economy Past and Present" in May 1934, Heckscher endeavoured to set economic planning tendencies in a long historical perspective, taking the mediaeval system and mercantilism as his starting point. It was true in principle that mercantilism opposed coercion and state production. "But neither of these extremely important reservations can prevent the aims of mercantilism from being regarded as an expression for a kind of planned economy. In fact, however, the realization of this idea was mainly a task for future generations to realize". Liberalism became the "executor" of mercantilism and swept away almost all traces of the medieval dissolution; thus, it was liberalism which represented economic planning, even though the plan was the reverse of state intervention. Liberalism set enormous productive forces free which in turn put it at risk. "Here we have the old story of Frankenstein, who created the monster to which he himself fell a victim".[124] Heckscher saw two primary factors:

---

[121]B. Ohlin, "Nya vindar i U.S.A.?", *Stockholms-Tidningen*, May 2, 1934.

[122]B. Ohlin, "Roosevelts industripolitik", *Stockholms-Tidningen*, July 19, 1934.

[123]Dagens Nyheter, "Konjunkturen konfronterad med politiken. Planhushållningens troende och tvivlare i debatt", *Dagens Nyheter*, May 12, 1934.

[124]E. Heckscher, "Planned Economy Past and Present", *Index*, månadsskrift utgiven av Svenska Handelsbanken IX(5) (1934): 96–97, 99.

One is the superiority, as regards both technique and organization, of big scale industry over operations on a smaller scale [...]. Moreover, side by side with the great technical and economic units there arose something else, having the same and perhaps still more widespread effects, namely, the ubiquitous systems of conduits or pipe-lines all controlled from central points: lines for forwarding spiritual and material communications, such as telegraphs, telephones and railways, gas, electricity for both power and light, water, drainage and many others of the most indispensable requirements of modern life. [---] But it is only the experience gained in quite recent times that has brought into sharp relief the hazardous consequences that the development of "Frankenstein's monster" has had in quite a different way, viz. – that of actually *enhancing the power of the State*.[125]

Heckscher concluded that "there can be no doubt that the actual situation so far implies a strengthening of the executive's resources to a degree hitherto unknown in history" and this opened the "prospect that the individuals in a state will become its slaves, if efforts are not made to ward off the danger".[126] Heckscher also pursued an argument concerning the risk of misjudgements. In a centrally regulated economy, a mistake has greater consequences. The number of mistakes may, on the other hand, be fewer because the state has an overview which individual firms that are independent of one another lack.

In June, the Swedish economic elite convened at the yearly Chamber of Commerce meeting. Gustaf Åkerman was the main speaker and his theme was contemporary tendencies in Swedish economic policy. He focused on policies regarding wages, agriculture and business cycle and said that they all unfortunately tended towards central planning. Planning was difficult in a world of constantly moving targets. Individuals changed their targets continuously according to a changing reality in order to avoid losses. Governments did not care as much about losses. Targets fixed by governments were consequently realized "in a rather insensitive and inflexible way and without being subject to continuous adjustment". "Because of this, government planning has a

---

[125]Ibid., 99–100.
[126]Ibid., 102.

natural and inherent tendency, often felt in a palpable way, to be hostile towards both freedom and development".[127]

Planning or Progress?

Cassel continued his offensive against planning during the summer and autumn of 1934. In an article in the *American Bankers Association Journal* in July, he explained that liberalism is a system of planning, using competition to attain the highest efficiency, and that "Planned Economy" is a duplication of terms:

> "Economy" in itself means a planned coordination of efforts towards a satisfaction of wants. It is natural enough that people who lack economic education should feel a need of a personification of such planning, just as primitive people have always loved to have their ideas represented by some personality, be it a human being or an ox.[128]

The sequence of events leading to demands for planning was described in the following way: The state had failed to exert its basic economic function, to provide an orderly monetary system. Prices were pushed down through a process of deflation. Producers, burdened with debts, saw themselves brought to ruin and turned to the state for help. In popular belief, low prices were the result of foreign competition. There was thus a demand for protection. Protectionism affected domestic industries in different ways. The state became involved in a gradually increasing regulation of the entire economic life. "All these efforts obviously needed to be coordinated in a rational way, and thus the demand for a planning authority became stronger day by day".[129] The only way

---

[127]*20:de svenska handelskammarmötet i Borås den 18 och 19 juni 1934: Protokoll och handlingar* (Stockholm: K.L. Beckmans Boktryckeri, 1934), 10. The lecture got attention in Svenska Dagbladet, "Handelskammarmötet dryftar näringspolitiken. Planhushållningen utdömes av professor G. Åkerman", *Svenska Dagbladet*, June 19, 1934.

[128]G. Cassel, "Planned Economy", *American Bankers Association Journal* 26(July) (1934): 15.

[129]Ibid., 16.

out went through a recovery of private enterprise. Such a recovery was, however, impossible as long as the monetary system was not stabilized and as long as governments continued to interfere and restrict the freedom of private enterprise.

> But as progress in its general sense is a most important cause of disturbances in economic life and of the dynamic conditions in which it finds itself continually involved, it is naturally easy enough to prove that we would have much greater stability if we were prepared to sacrifice all progress. This sacrifice is of course not made consciously by the advocates of a planned economy, and at any rate they do not tell the public that this would be the tremendous price humanity would have to pay for the stability they promise as the fruit of their planning.[130]

Without growth, poverty. Cassel asserted that "real want as a mass phenomenon with hungry and freezing millions occurs mainly in countries with a 'planned economy'". Reduced mobility, not least reduced migration, was a major problem. Cassel did not accept the idea of a closed western frontier. There was plenty of room for migrants in the United States and Canada. Previous migration had been a "precious gift from abroad", the shutdown of migration had been "one of the gravest mistakes in US economic policy" and "[t]he punishment [had] arrived with a crisis of unparalleled strength".[131]

In a speech in Oslo, in the presence of the royal family and members of the Norwegian government, Cassel explained that economic planning would require an infallible reason but in reality had proven to be absolutely planless. He sketched losses of economic, political and spiritual freedom, leading to absolute dictatorship. A newspaper report from the occasion stated that Cassel's speech was met not with applause but with thunder of approval.[132]

---

[130]Ibid., 15. It should be noted that economic progress (growth) was a key element in Cassel's economic thought, displayed, for example, in *The Theory of Social Economy* (London: T. Fisher Unwin, 1923).

[131]G. Cassel, "Arbetslöshet och kolonisation", *Svenska Dagbladet*, September 20, 1934.

[132]Arg., "Cassel viser oss den enkle vei ut av krisen og vanviddet: Fast prisnivå, faste valutakurser", *Aftenposten*, October 5, 1934.

Ohlin increasingly focused on party politics and argued that the Liberal Party must free itself from the "fear of any planned state intervention", which could be noticed in some Liberal newspapers. Twentieth-century liberalism, primarily designed in Britain, was something quite different from the old nineteenth-century liberalism. At the same time, one had to watch out for Social Democratic ambitions to increase the influence of government for its own sake.[133]

In the election campaign during the fall, Arvid Lindman, leader of the Conservative Party, spoke of "the modern idolization of the state" and of "a fantastic blind faith in the capacity of the state to step in and put everything right". He sounded a warning against a three-stage development—crisis policy, planned economy, socialization—and wondered what a planned economy would look like in a country like Sweden, where so many people were employed in export industries dependent on conditions in the world market, and in agriculture dependent on "weather and wind and the beneficence of the Lord".[134]

When Prime Minister Hansson spoke of the need for more government control over the machinery of production, Cassel replied that governments, having destroyed the monetary system, bore the entire responsibility for the contemporary economic disaster. In an attempt to correct the problem they had caused, governments had intervened in economic life, not least in international trade, and in the process created unemployment of incomparable proportions. Cassel pointed to economic misfortunes in Britain and the US. The British coal mining industry had declined due to increased use of water power and oil in other countries. How could a socialist government with full control over this industry have prevented this decline? The US banking crisis was due to many small banks lacking resources and management. This was an effect of legislation intended to prevent the emergence of big banks. Furthermore, government intervention in the banking sector during the crisis had not been successful since the credits to private businesses had continued to shrink.[135]

---

[133]B. Ohlin, "Folkpartiet, liberalismen och framtiden", *Stockholms-Tidningen*, October 23, 1934.

[134]A. Lindman, *Vår svenska väg: Urval av tal i 1934 års valrörelse* (Ulricehamn, 1934), 86, 105.

[135]G. Cassel, "Socialismens misstag", *Svenska Dagbladet*, November 10, 1934.

Cassel once more brought up the issue of dictatorships. Dictators had proved to be victims of the same economic delusions as ordinary people and had put these delusions into grand scale action. The political colour of the dictatorships was of minor importance. Leaders in Germany, the US and Russia were all incapable of understanding the workings of the monetary system and the conditions vital for economic progress. Militaries were assigned to control price formation, "the finest regulator of economic life". Cassel in particular attacked a Swedish political scientist and right-winger, Adrian Molin, who was sympathetic to German National Socialism. He dismissed German economic policy as a good example of "quackery" but above all condemned Nazism as a denial of values fundamental in any culture of a higher standing, values like the rule of law and freedom. In Sweden, these values were an indispensable part of the national cultural heritage. Cassel admitted that he was critical of some tendencies in Swedish society, but this criticism was certainly not intended to open the door to any dictatorial influences of German or Russian nature. The intention was to safeguard freedom and rule of law in Sweden and in this respect Sweden had only one natural ally: Britain. "We must join the best and wisest forces in Britain and – in a fight against tendencies towards economic planning and dictatorship which can be seen there also – strive for a sensible restoration of the world economic order and thereby for increased wealth of nations".[136]

Heckscher's Great Showdown

Heckscher's great showdown with the advocates of economic planning came in November 1934, when he delivered an address on the subject to the Economic Society and clashed with the younger economists Myrdal, Ohlin, and Kock.

Heckscher began by describing the planned economy as a "planless command economy", characterized more by compulsion and central direction than by plan; as far as planning was concerned, the market

---

[136]G. Cassel, "Sverige och diktaturerna", *Svenska Dagbladet*, November 14, 1934.

economy could "lay claim to the name of 'economic planning' with at least as much justification".[137] He said that he would not seek to conceal in which direction his own sympathies were to be found – an unnecessary admission, it seems – and taunted his younger colleagues as "apostles of the planned economy": "Their nostrils are filled with the new air to the point where they seem to be in no condition to breathe any other".[138]

Heckscher outlined the developments which in his opinion had created an unprecedented scope for state direction—large-scale production, diminished elbow-room for geographical expansion, a stationary population, and modern "distributary systems"; "[h]umanity is woven into a network of lines which are controlled from central points"[139]— and depicted the dangers which threatened if economic planning was put into practice:

1. The dynamic factor, technology, would be checked. People normally defend themselves against changes which threaten their established positions. In a state-directed economy, it is easier to prevent such changes than it is in a free market. In practice too, nine out of ten interventions on the part of the state turned out to be aimed at "propping up what has already become superfluous".[140] Attempts to vitalize the economy through interventions had done more harm than good; in Sweden, the economic turnaround had begun before a countercyclical programme had even been formulated and interventions would anyway only have a short-term impact:

> The interventions bear the same characteristics as the kind of medical treatment which used to be applied by market horse-traders with old nags for sale. They gave them half a stoup of aquavit to make them pirouette as they had done in the springtime of their youth, only to revert, of course, to their former sloth once the intoxication wore off.[141]

---

[137]Nationalekonomiska Föreningen, "Planhushållning", November 20, 1934, 145–146.
[138]Ibid., 153.
[139]Ibid., 151.
[140]Ibid., 159.
[141]Ibid., 160.

2. The planned economy was incompatible with democracy in the long run. Democracy's political compromises were by nature far removed from planning. It is true that even a dictator must make concessions to the social forces that back him up. "But the dictator at least has the possibility of getting his own way, without incessant compromises with leading politicians or party groups".[142]

3. Personal freedom would be restricted, especially for the workers. In a state-directed economy, it would be impossible to "leave the incomparably most important cost element in production to the free play of forces or to independent organizations". "It is out of the question that the state would be able to tolerate even for a moment trade unions or consumers' cooperative unions of the sort we know now".[143]

4. The conditions of "spiritual" (intellectual) life would be fundamentally changed by virtue of the fact that the state controlled the media and could fill them "to the brim with the spirit desired by the powers that be and no other".[144]

Myrdal was the first discussant. He stated that the "horrifying depiction" of a disorganized, planless and forced economy which Heckscher had outlined had nothing to do with economic planning. "[A]s far as I know, only he himself and a few individuals practically and theoretically close to him use the term 'economic planning' in this sense". Heckscher had erroneously "got it into his head that some of his colleagues had a sadistic love of compulsion for compulsion's sake, regardless of how judiciously it is planned". Economic planning was, according to Myrdal, not what the world had witnessed during the ongoing crisis. Its ambition was to increase economic mobility, to "achieve an adjustment, which in the stagnant liberal economy apparently does not happen spontaneously, and protect social interest, which

---

[142]Ibid., 164.

[143]Ibid., 165. It seems that Heckscher in this case contradicts himself, for earlier in his speech he said this: "Liberalism accepted both individual and state, what it rejected was the formations which appeared between individual and state". Ibid., 147.

[144]Ibid., 166.

otherwise will be lost". Myrdal thus saw economic planning as something vague and for the moment non-existent. This was duly noted by discussants representing the business community like Ruben Rausing and Marcus Wallenberg. Rausing said that he had expected to hear of a programme from "one of the leading apostles of economic planning", but no such programme had been presented, possibly because "no such program exists".[145]

Kock pointed to developments in Britain, where depressed areas had ended up in a cumulative process of unemployment, increasing taxation and deteriorating markets for local industries, which caused industries to move out, which led to a new round of unemployment, etc. Wouldn't it in such a case be wise to plan the location of industries?

Ohlin found the term economic planning unfortunate since all economic activity is planned. "People always try to economize with the future in mind". Just like Myrdal, he accused Heckscher of having painted "an extreme picture of some sort of mystical, extreme command economy" which had no supporters in Sweden. The real question was to what degree the economy ought to be centrally directed. In view of the tendencies Heckscher had outlined—large-scale businesses, stagnant population, technological change—he posed the following questions: *"is it not likely that we should adapt our organizational apparatus according to these conditions?"* "Is it not likely that this [liberal] 19th century construction is no longer suitable, and that a certain modification, a gradual change, is needed?"[146]

Ohlin wished to discuss different types of public sector activities instead of a cliché like economic planning. He mentioned state and municipal enterprise, "framework planning", control intended to avoid abuse and business cycle policy. Framework planning was portrayed in the following words: "The public sector attempts through legislation but also in other ways to draw a frame, within which private businessmen and enterprises can more or less take care of themselves".[147] He was

---

[145]Ibid., 167, 172–173, 178.
[146]Ibid., 181–182, 185.
[147]Ibid., 183.

flabbergasted by Heckscher's prophecy of an imminent danger of dictatorship—such a process would probably take about 50 years.[148]

"It appears to me", retorted Heckscher, as "an excessively naive view of events to look only at the details and judge every individual issue by itself". He was surprised that Myrdal and Ohlin had shied away from a discussion of principles. He declared that one must be clear about the direction in which events are running and decide whether one wants them to go any further or not. There was a special gibe for Myrdal: "Sadistic is certainly an ugly word, but I do not believe there can be the least doubt that there are people who do have a love of compulsion". Against Ohlin's timing of possible dictatorship, he delivered an apt rejoinder: "If we do not get any such [dictatorship] the next 50 years, we will never get it, but – I wish to add – if we get it in the next couple of years, we may not get rid of it in 50 years".[149]

Certainly there is an interventionist tendency in economic policy, replied Ohlin, but does this not result from external circumstances, from the depression? Isn't it better to make minor interventions in order to avoid major dangers? Experiences from other countries demonstrated that, for example, if no interventions were made on behalf of farmers, they could take the Nazi road. In his final statement, Heckscher arrives at the conclusion—just as Bagge had—that the spirit underlying intervention is crucial: "The question is whether the tendency of our present policy is not influenced by a certain degree of preconceived intent. Is not the tendency influenced, for example, by the fact that those in charge of policy are socialists by birth and force of habit?"[150] Myrdal had the last word. He sided with Ohlin in saying that nations which had not taken action against crises in time had been forced into coercive measures. He was apparently very upset since he asked the other participants if the Economic Society was intended to be a platform for market liberal propaganda.

---

[148]50 years from the debate means 1984. Fifteen years after the debate, George Orwell published his famous novel *1984*.
[149]Nationalekonomiska Föreningen, "Planhushållning", 190–191.
[150]Ibid., 200.

Myrdal and Ohlin thus refuted Heckscher along three lines: (1) It is meaningless to discuss such a cliché concept as economic planning; one ought instead to discuss specific practical problems. (2) If the conditions of the liberal order has changed, the organization of economic life must be adapted accordingly. (3) If deliberate interventions are not launched in time, there is a risk of falling into situations that really demand coercive interventions. Heckscher on his part wished to discuss the drift into economic planning in his own time and the ideas behind it, the prerequisites for planning and the possible consequences of it.

The debate was followed up by Ohlin in an editorial, in which he wrote that both a strictly centrally directed and a completely free economy were unthinkable. The real issue concerned the limits and forms of central direction. He found it "sensational" that Heckscher in the debate had disassociated himself from Manchester liberalism and, as several times before, he concluded that the task ahead was not to scrap crisis policy but to "rationalize and coordinate and constantly adapt it to changing conditions with more consideration to effects in the long run".[151]

When Heckscher published an extended version of his address as a paper under the title "Command Economy and 'Planned Economy'"—characterized by Lewin as "one of the most acute and lucid right-wing contributions to the planned economy debate of the 1930s"[152]—he had added a further dangerous effect of the planned economy: nationalism, not to say autarky. Trade and industry cannot be directed from a central point over a greater area than that controlled by a state. International economic intercourse cannot be centrally directed. Of course, states can negotiate with one another, but every business transaction simultaneously becomes a political act associated with prestige considerations. Economic planners become, willy-nilly, economic nationalists. Planners in one country cannot control planners in other countries, and the result is that they all attempt to reduce the disturbances emanating from international trade.[153]

---

[151]B. Ohlin, "Hushållning och anpassning", *Stockholms-Tidningen*, November 22, 1934.

[152]Lewin, *Planhushållningsdebatten*, 125.

[153]E. Heckscher, *Tvångshushållning och "planhushållning* (Stockholm: Kooperativa Förbundets Bokförlag, 1934). Heckscher's booklet made its mark in the debate on planning. An editorial in *Dagens Nyheter*, for example, quoted it extensively and used it to attack the Mammoth inquiry

Population and Relation Crises

In the autumn of 1934, Gunnar and Alva Myrdal triggered a hot debate with their book on the population issue.[154] This book strained the relations between Cassel/Heckscher and Gunnar Myrdal even more than hitherto. Cassel took on the book in articles, later on published in a book on "Life or Death".[155] He praised the Myrdals for having raised the issue but condemned them for using it to argue for a communist society.[156] The Myrdals doubted that the word communism could be used to scare educated readers, in the same way as the chimney sweeper had been used to frighten children in the old days. They concluded that Cassel, "the great authority of liberal conservatism", was empty-handed and could only "repeat old invocations".[157] Cassel retorted that the reforms suggested by the Myrdals meant "a radical socialist production system under a regime of government planning" and that the term communist was appropriate since the Myrdals wished to socialize not only production but also consumption.[158]

Heckscher and his wife Ebba attacked the Myrdals even more fiercely. The Myrdals' arguments were splendid and sharp-witted but at the same time characterized by fanaticism and used as "the crowbar with which to turn obdurate Swedish society upside-down".[159] The result was an immediate crisis in the relations between the Myrdals and the Heckschers. Alva wrote letters accusing the Heckschers of "cheap

---

(see below) which was said to "expedite the pioneer work for the 'economic planning' many yearn for". See Dagens Nyheter, "Demokratins framtid", *Dagens Nyheter*, January 7, 1935.

[154]A. Myrdal and G. Myrdal, *Kris i befolkningsfrågan* (Stockholm: Bonniers, 1934).

[155]G. Cassel, *Liv eller död* (Stockholm: Albert Bonniers Förlag, 1935).

[156]G. Cassel, "Vårt folks livsfråga", *Svenska Dagbladet*, November 25, 1934 and "Samhällsintresset i befolkningsfrågan", *Svenska Dagbladet*, November 27, 1934.

[157]A. Myrdal and G. Myrdal, "Avfolkning eller samhällsreform", *Svenska Dagbladet*, December 6, 1934.

[158]G. Cassel, "Svar till Myrdals", *Svenska Dagbladet*, December 9, 1934.

[159]E. Heckscher and E. Heckscher, "Befolkningsfrågan som murbräcka", *Dagens Nyheter*, December 5, 1934 and "Familjen i stöpsleven", *Dagens Nyheter*, December 7, 1934.

counterfeiting" and Gunnar wrote of "*cheap* dialectics", declaring that having spent seven years studying law, he knew how to "scrutinize words and distinguish arguments from advocacy".[160] Heckscher replied by wondering whether Gunnar was not "lacking in scholarly temperament and so ought to find his chief employment as an agitator". He regretted that his criticisms had been too detailed—"the book ought to have been exploded as a constructive whole".[161]

In early 1935, Ohlin once more saw liberalism standing at the crossroads. He now wrote of three different outlooks: the old liberal *laissez-faire* type, the social liberalism which sees government's role as depending upon current circumstances, and Marxist state socialism advocating a complete government takeover. At this point, when crisis policy was being dismantled and the question revolved around more permanent long-term measures, the scenario differed from the previous one. "It is between this [state socialist] outlook on the one hand and the social, active liberalism on the other that in practice the most important dividing line will be drawn in our country".[162]

> There is an attempt from Social Democratic quarters to portray a long-term state socialism, for instance in the shape of extensive monopolization, as a continuation of the business cycle and crisis policy which has been successfully pursued the last couple of years. These are however two completely different things. Business cycle policy cannot be used to warrant a state socialist monopoly and control policy.

When the Swedish government in early 1935 launched the so-called Mammoth investigation,[163] and Prime Minister Hansson stated that

---

[160]Letters from Alva Myrdal to the Heckschers December 11, 12, and 14, 1934 and from Gunnar Myrdal (undated) in Heckscher's collection of letters at the Royal Library in Stockholm.

[161]Letter from Heckscher to Myrdal 18 December 1934. Myrdal in a letter of April 13, 1935, made a far-reaching attempt to repair his relation to Heckscher, who, on April 14, somewhat grudgingly took the extended hand.

[162]B. Ohlin, "Fronten mot statssocialismen", *Stockholms-Tidningen*, January 20, 1935.

[163]The committee was appointed around new year 1934/35 and its report delivered in late 1935: *Betänkande om folkförsörjning och arbetsfred*, Part I–II (Stockholm: Isaac Marcus Boktryckeriaktiebolag, 1935) (SOU, 1935: 65–66).

the purpose was to "regulate economic conflicts of interest" and to "secure the normal pace of production and a balanced national supply of goods", Cassel questioned whether politicians knew what they were doing. The problem to be solved, asserted Cassel, is "manifestly nothing less than the general problem of pricing". Such an undertaking must lead "to an investigation of the very foundations of the entire national economy and thus also to a general rationalization of all state intervention".[164] In order to gain anything at all from state intervention in free economic life, said Cassel, the state must keep "within the framework of the price mechanism", "establish a clear and consistent goal for its policy", and "arrange all its measures rationally to this purpose".[165]

Cassel again suggested that ever more state intervention would mean that parliament would face difficulties which would put democracy in danger. Firstly, the democratic process was too slow to be able to guide the economy through its business cycles and ever-changing conditions. Secondly, the economy was so complicated that the parliament would be overstrained. Thirdly, when the government could not rely on an absolute majority in parliament, every decision would have to be reached through compromise, and there would be no consistency between different decisions. The consequence would be "the most dreadful thing: *a planned economy without a plan*".[166]

> The difficulties and hazards for private industry will increase endlessly and the sense of insecurity will be so far-reaching that business life will be increasingly paralyzed. [...] As a consequence there will be never-ending state intervention and state control [...]. [Those] who at any cost wish to implement a planned economy must be prepared to sacrifice the parliamentary form of government and the entire democratic system. In many countries this has already happened.

---

[164]G. Cassel, "Statsingripandets rationalisering", *Svenska Dagbladet*, February 10, 1935.

[165]G. Cassel, "Borgerlighetens prövostund", *Svenska Dagbladet*, February 22, 1935.

[166]G. Cassel, "Folkrepresentation och planhushållning", *Svenska Dagbladet*, March 8, 1935.

However, Cassel had a modest and constructive proposal. In other countries, economic councils had been appointed and this model ought to be applied in Sweden also. This council should contain economic expertise and have an independent status, and thus not be influenced by "the gusts of day-to-day politics". "We need a permanent body which can analyze economic problems independently and express its opinion, and which the government must always listen to before submitting its proposals to the *Riksdag*". In this way, the political system would achieve "a substantially higher rationality and efficiency in its work". Cassel suggested that this organ should be named the "Central Economic Inquiry" (*Centrala ekonomiska utredningen*), be appointed by the government with some assistance from the *Riksdag* (through electors) and be equipped with a permanent secretariat.[167]

Cassel at the same time attacked the Swedish agricultural policy in the same manner as Heckscher had done in 1930 when he commented upon an investigation into grain production. He could not find "any clear objective for agricultural policy as a whole" but "a perfectly scary picture of planlessness, shortsightedness and lack of ability to understand even the simplest relations in economic life".[168] Authorities had created "an incredible muddle [...] in their eagerness to appear as the savior of agriculture". He referred to his "Central Economic Inquiry" proposal and, in his justification of it, came close to the coordination argument advocated by planners: "The only way to end this [planless] system is to enforce a *coherent* treatment of all major issues under the common point of view of the national economy".[169]

---

[167]G. Cassel, "En centralekonomisk utredning", *Svenska Dagbladet*, March 13, 1935. Salter had outlined such a council in *Planhushållning* 1934. In view of the discord among economists at the time, such a council would have had problems agreeing.

[168]G. Cassel, "Planlös jordbrukspolitik", *Sunt Förnuft* 15(March) (1935): 57–58.

[169]G. Cassel, "Hushållning", *Sunt Förnuft* 15(May) (1935): 131.

The Battle of Oslo

In June 1935, economists from the Nordic countries convened in Oslo. Economic planning was one of the topics on the agenda. Norwegian economist Wilhelm Keilhau delivered the introduction. He started out by saying that he disagreed 100% with Myrdal's position in the 1934 debate in the Swedish Economic Society, that a discussion about planning must revolve around concrete matters and details. Keilhau wished to discuss principles.

Keilhau noted that the term planned economy originates from Friedrich Engels and constitutes the second step of the Marxist scheme: "first socialization of the material means of production, then planned economic management". However, during the world economic crisis, politicians in capitalist countries had begun to use the term independently of its Marxist origin. "The term 'planned economy' has become everyman's property". All economies were, of course, based on planning. "Without planning, no economy". However, in a capitalist society "each individual has the right to undertake economic planning. Marxists demand state monopoly on economic planning. That's the difference". Furthermore, current capitalist societies were not anarchic since the laws of the workings of the price mechanism could be expressed in "unambiguous mathematic formulas".[170]

A fully implemented planned economy could also make use of the price mechanism. This was the case in Soviet Russia and "if the first five-year plan can pride itself of some success, it is to a large extent due to the use of the price mechanism". The difference between a planned and a market society was that in the former, the price mechanism was used as a means of force. This force was executed by bureaucrats and their only option was to simplify and standardize production, which meant less consumption choice and a lower standard of living. "On the whole, a transition from an economy determined by demand to a national planned economy expressed in terms of political ideology must be seen as a bureaucratic revolution". Capitalists acted in "the spirit of

---

[170]*Forhandlinger ved det tiende nordiske nasjonaløkonomiske møte i Oslo den 17–19 juni 1935.* "Kritisk vurdering av planøkonomien" (Oslo: Grøndahl & Søns Boktrykkeri, 1935), 13–14.

profit", bureaucrats in previous societies had acted in "the spirit of service" but in Marxist, fascist and Nazi societies, they acted in "the spirit of the party". This spirit could not be reconciled with parliamentarism. "Nobody, who in his heart embraces political freedom and political democracy, can therefore advocate a totally planned economy".[171]

And so Keilhau went on. A planned economy could not allow organizational freedom. It would be hostile to trade unions. This explained why intellectual academics, but not trade union leaders, agitated for planning. Planners must also take control of foreign trade. Economic conflicts between countries would then turn into political conflicts. "From a pacifist point of view 'the planned economy' is thus a dangerous system".[172] After this salvo, Keilhau went on to discuss whether his arguments against full-scale planning could be applied to separate state interventions.

In the following debate, Ohlin appeared as the first discussant. He had enjoyed the latter part of Keilhau's speech, when particular problems were discussed, but claimed not to understand the notion of a totally planned economy. He objected to Keilhau's depiction of production determined by demand in a capitalist society since "between people's needs and effective demand stands unequal income distribution and periodical income disruptions for some people". Ohlin pointed to contemporary tendencies, such as large-scale production, new means of communication and reduced opportunities for migration, and insisted that "we need to adapt organizational modes to these shifting preconditions". He mentioned state enterprise, social insurance, tariffs, agricultural and business cycle policies, all elements of his "framework" economy, and assumed that everybody could agree that these activities should be pursued in a planned manner. He labelled Keilhau's concern over interventions in the price mechanism a "Manchester liberal atavism" and ended up with a forceful accusation: "It is Manchester liberal diehards, opposing all state interventions, who prepare the ground for dictatorship and communism".[173] Keilhau strongly objected to Ohlin's

---

[171]Ibid., 16, 19, 21.

[172]Ibid., 21.

[173]Ibid., 34–35, 38.

depiction of him as a Manchester liberal. That type of liberalism was long gone. One could not in 1935 attack something which had disappeared in the 1860s. Ohlin countered by maliciously expressing admiration of the fact that Norway was so much before its time.

Heckscher objected to Ohlin's view of new preconditions, a view he had himself expressed several times. Employment within agriculture and industry decreased or stagnated, whereas employment within trade and communications increased. These developments were conducive to small-scale production and increased mobility. Increased income per capita meant a shift in the hierarchy of needs. There was consequently need for more flexibility. "This means, as I see it, even if it may sound paradoxical, that what we call a planned economy [...] is an *outdated* phenomenon".[174] Ohlin objected by saying that it was most desirable to reduce variations in consumption.

One participant noted that planning failures in the US and Soviet Union were often excused for having been "clumsily executed". Kock intervened to defend Roosevelt's policies. Her main argument was that US conditions in 1935 must be compared to conditions in 1933, and not 1928 as some debaters preferred. To imagine that America was heading towards state socialism was to "see ghosts in broad daylight".[175]

Leif Björk, a Swedish Ph.D. student, focused on the distinction between economic planning in capitalist and socialist societies. In a capitalist society, planners had to take capitalist claims to profits into account, which set narrow limits to their ambitions to increase production and consumption. In the Soviet Union, there had never been any general difficulty to dispose of production. A Norwegian participant suggested that young Swedish economists had arrived in Oslo "with their heads filled with Swedish crisis planning" and did not understand that Norway was on the verge of real Soviet style planning.[176]

---

[174]Ibid., 51.

[175]Ibid., 74.

[176]Ibid., 76. Björk had off and on 1928–1932 visited the Soviet Union on a scholarship from the Economic Society and was impressed by what he saw. In 1935, he submitted an essay on economic planning with Bagge as his supervisor. See A. I-n, "Ryska bondsöner läsa i brigader, läraren konsult", *Dagens Nyheter*, October 4, 1931; and R. von Euler and J. Hagberg, "Leif Björk", *Dagens Nyheter*, July 4, 2000.

The Oslo meeting resulted in a final breakdown in the relation between Heckscher and Ohlin. Heckscher had for some time been frustrated by Ohlin's frequent leaves of absence from teaching duties at the Stockholm School of Economics. After their clash in Oslo, Heckscher in a letter expressed concerns that Ohlin's "propensity to be open to everything" meant "that people presently in power will be able to get you along with almost anything". Ohlin was chairman of the Liberal Party's youth organization, but Heckscher suggested that he ought instead to sign up as member of the Social Democratic Party. Ohlin's answer came in a letter six weeks later. He claimed to be a mainstream liberal, unlike Heckscher, who had little interest in poor people and social reforms and in reality belonged to the Conservative Party. He added that Heckscher had a political bent which sometimes made him do "less honest things". Heckscher's reply was short. He said his own letter had been inappropriate, that Ohlin's letter had felt embarrassing and that in spite of this he hoped that they would be able to uphold their professional duties.[177] Somewhat later, Heckscher announced that their personal relation was finished and Ohlin concluded that they had agreed on "collegial treatment".[178] Heckscher's relations with both Ohlin and Myrdal were now frozen.[179]

Liberal Planning

At the same time as his conflict with Heckscher culminated, Ohlin directed his interest towards Britain, first towards a plan for a new economic policy designed by Lloyd George with the help of a large number of experts, among them Keynes and Walter Layton,[180] and thereafter

---

[177]Letter from Heckscher to Ohlin June 21, from Ohlin to Heckscher August 3 and from Heckscher to Ohlin August 8, 1935.

[178]Letter from Heckscher to Ohlin September 1 and from Ohlin to Heckscher September 5, 1935. In a letter of August 20, Heckscher wrote: "None of my disciples have interested me as much as you, I have not gone out of my way as much for anybody else – and nobody else has caused me such disappointment".

[179]More on this conflict in S.-E. Larsson, *Bertil Ohlin* (Stockholm: Atlantis, 1996).

[180]B. Ohlin, "Lloyd George contra Chamberlain", *Stockholms-Tidningen*, July 31, 1935.

towards a British "five year plan" (The Next Five Years) presented by a large number of experts from different ideological camps. Ohlin was very pleased with the five year plan. It was not aimed at more intervention in economic life but rather at "a rational coordination of the ones already in place". To this end, the establishment of an economic "general staff" was recommended. If different measures were coordinated, this would create an improved environment for business. The whole plan was very much in line with Ohlin's own agenda: "Those who are behind this political work in England to a large extent belong to liberal circles. Their basic view is a social liberalism closely corresponding to the one which more and more seems to dominate the Swedish Liberal Party [...]."[181]

When the Minister of Education, Arthur Engberg, spoke of contemporary government threats against "spiritual freedom", Cassel raised a question: How could this plea for freedom be reconciled with Social Democrats' "constant pursuit of government guardianship over business life or absolute subordination of individuals under trade unions or other coercive organizations"? This time, he used historical materialism as a springboard: "In the long run a nation's mentality – especially according to Marxist opinion – must be influenced to a considerable degree by the economic conditions under which it works". Personal and intellectual freedom had rested on the foundations of the economic freedom of merchants and farmers. A command economy, which reduced the individual to "the well-disciplined servant of an immense bureaucracy", would demolish the foundations of this freedom.[182]

An editorial in *Social-Demokraten* questioned whether Cassel could be ignorant of how matters stood with the freedom of farmers and merchants under the prevailing "regime of high capitalism". The farmers were in the hands of capitalist banks. It was only with the help of the Social Democratic movement and of their own organizations that industrial workers had succeeded in breaking out of "the condition of slavery in which they found themselves during the happy and glorious

---

[181]B. Ohlin, "En engelsk femårsplan utan partifärg", *Stockholms-Tidningen*, August 16, 1935.

[182]G. Cassel, "Andlig frihet och ekonomisk", *Svenska Dagbladet*, August 25, 1935.

days of the acclaimed liberal nineteenth century economy". "There are so many other kinds of freedom", the newspaper concluded, "than Manchester liberalism's formal freedom to smash your competitors and sell at the highest possible price".[183]

At a major business exhibition (*Arosmässan*, a yearly event since 1907), Ohlin was the main speaker and presented his "liberal economic planning" as an alternative to state socialist planning. He spoke of increased labour mobility, planning of infrastructure and housing and the need for better economic statistics, things he would elaborate in great detail in a book one year later (see below). At the following dinner, Minister of Trade Fritjof Ekman more or less associated himself with what Ohlin had said.[184]

When Ohlin commented upon the "Mammoth investigation", he delivered both blame and praise. The investigation had been assigned to look at relations between different interests and their relations to the state. The question was whether government through its many interventions would attempt to determine a just and reasonable distribution of income. Before the war, many pundits had figured that income distribution must be decided by "the free play of forces", by price formation. The depression had discredited this posture. What would have happened to Swedish agriculture without government support? On the other hand, there was a more or less common understanding that government cannot decide what constitutes a "just" income distribution. Ohlin praised the investigation for being "almost an encyclopedia on Sweden's economic policy", but blamed it for not taking into consideration that "regulation might mean stagnation".[185]

In a 1935 Christmas discourse, Cassel took up the issue which Heckscher and Ohlin had dealt with as a prerequisite for planning— larger production units—but adopted a completely different point of view. To reduce production costs through large-scale production, producers must have a colossal outlet and recruit a broad segment of the

---

[183]Social-Demokraten, "Staten och friheten", *Social-Demokraten*, August 26, 1935.
[184]Dagens Nyheter, "Sysselsättningsfrågan dryftas på Arosmässan. Liberal planhushållning skulle göra susen, menar professor Ohlin", *Dagens Nyheter*, November 3, 1935.
[185]B. Ohlin, "Mammututredningens dilemma", *Stockholms-Tidningen*, December 22, 1935.

population as customers. Ford had to recruit craftsmen and cookers as customers and mass-produced clothing eliminated visible signs of class difference. "It is in the nature of contemporary capitalism that it is forced to serve democracy in this way".[186]

In 1936, the Social Democratic government decided to launch an investigation into which public works could be mobilized in case of another economic downturn. Ohlin cautioned that "the most important preparation for bad times is wise restraint in good times!" He was not impressed by Social Democratic claims that economic crises are always caused by "bourgeois society". Would international conflicts and fluctuating foreign demand disappear if Sweden was socialized? The Social Democrats tried to blur the difference between business cycle policy and socialization policy.[187]

A Devil's Delusion

In an address in March 1936 accompanied by a paper titled "Private Trade and Industry in a Time of Command Economy", Heckscher attempted to view economic planning tendencies in a short-term historical perspective, taking the World War as his starting point. Wartime controls had had effects in opposing directions. On the one hand, they had created a general distaste for state intervention. On the other hand, they had strengthened private monopoly; the assistance of industrialists had been invoked in order to implement the controls, and their associations had taken advantage of the opportunity to exclude those outside their membership from allocations of raw materials and fuel. The war had also given birth to violent nationalism, and from this followed an increased estimation of the state's loftiness and omnipotence. Nevertheless, he did not really consider the economic planning ideas which were gaining ground in the 1930s to be rooted in economic fact: "The suddenness of the changeover from one system to another precludes the possibility that

[186]G. Cassel, "Samhälleliga värden", *Sunt Förnuft* 15(Christmas) (1935): 404.

[187]B. Ohlin, "Krispolitik och socialism", *Stockholms-Tidningen*, January 19, 1936.

the direct cause had to a large extent been changes in the fundamental conditions of economic life". Such changes did not occur from day to day. It was therefore "inescapable that the sudden rise of the command economy has to be explained in terms of changed states of mind and policy rather than basic economic facts".[188]

Heckscher, however, soon modified his inescapable conclusion and admitted that the economy had, in fact, changed a great deal, and in a direction at odds with earlier economic theory. Above all, it was high unemployment that had triggered off much of the new policy. Heckscher's position seems a bit unclear, but it is based primarily on violent psychological fluctuations alongside economic ones. He reasoned thus: The crisis of 1920–1923 had been seen as a natural reaction to the dislocations of the war. The vigorous boom during the remainder of the 1920s had lent lustre to "the principles of free economic life" but when the 1930s crisis erupted, "all the previous prosperity was held to be its own opposite, a devil's delusion", and there ensued "a crisis of faith in the private economy as well".[189] Private business and industry, in other words, were on trial, and Heckscher accordingly turned to businessmen and industrialists with an admonition to brace up their self-discipline. It would not do to be opponents of state interference at one moment and accept state assistance to themselves at the next.

When a Swedish Liberal newspaper published an article, portraying Soviet planning as a model for the rest of the world, Cassel could hardly believe his eyes. "It is incomprehensible that a newspaper claiming some standard can serve its readers such a complete nonsense". During the first five-year plan, Russia had increased its stock of real capital through "a terrible reduction of the population's standard of living". During the second five-year plan, conditions had improved simply because Russia had reverted to a normal monetary system.[190]

Heckscher, in a debate in the Economic Society on government intervention and economic activity—the main speaker was Lionel Robbins—

---

[188]E. Heckscher, "Det privata näringslivet i tvångshushållningens tid", *Föredrag hållna inför svenska ekonomföreningen*, no. 1 (Stockholm, 1936), 15.

[189]Ibid., 12–13.

[190]G. Cassel, "Ryssland som mönster!" *Svenska Dagbladet*, April 25, 1936.

expressed deep scepticism about government ability to control business cycles. He declared business cycles to be "figments of the brain of economists and business people" and even if the cycle was known, it could not be controlled by politicians. He went so far as to say that "most of the discussions going on among theorists on this subject [economic policy] are much more appropriate to Jupiter and Saturn than to the small planet we live on".[191] When the issue of planned economy was taken up again by the Economic Society in a debate on "State Regulation of Trade and Industry", a graphic objection against planned economy was delivered by a Conservative, Karl Wistrand: state interventions are "equipped with barbs; they are easy to push in but painful to pull out".[192]

Cassel delivered a policy speech on "State and Economy" in which he found it natural that the scope of state undertakings was constantly widened, but, on the other hand, told his audience that strong economic growth had always occurred "in countries and at times when private entrepreneurship has been given maximum leeway and freedom".[193] In wide circles, expansion of state activity had become an end in itself.

> The final objective has been seen as a "planned economy", where all friction is eliminated, all shortcomings remedied, and the whole economy guided with the wisdom and perfection which could be expected from the highest Providence. This is however nothing but dogmatic faith, fully comparable to the worst superstitions which have previously possessed different aspects of human life.[194]

Planners, according to Cassel, often assumed that technological and economic progress had reached a stationary state but what was really to be expected was a duplication of the wealth of nations for every new generation. "Free price formation must therefore be constantly

[191]Nationalekonomiska Föreningen, "Government Expenditure and Economic Activity", March 23, 1936, 44.

[192]Nationalekonomiska Föreningen, "Statens regulering av næringslivet", May 4, 1936.

[193]G. Cassel, *Stat och näringsliv: Föredrag vid Hakonbolagets årsstämma 25 maj 1936* (Västerås: Hakonbolaget, 1936), 5.

[194]Ibid., 7.

operative and everywhere bring about the necessary adaption to constantly changing conditions during progress as fast as possible". Every random intervention in the process of price formation caused an endless series of disturbances. How this played out had been demonstrated by the "incredible chaos" created by Roosevelt's interventions. Another example was Swedish agricultural policy, "a muddle of interventions, the concerted effect of which nobody can foresee". Worst of all, the "political prices" tended to become articles of exchange in the general political horse-trade".[195]

> Wherever we are able to watch how government intervention in the economy unfolds, we will find that it is not guided by any plan, but that rather each issue is treated separately and is solved according to the prevailing political mode of power and with regard only to factors close at hand. When many issues are handled in this way, a real coordination of different interventions will never occur.[196]

In the election campaign of 1936, Prime Minister Hansson over the radio promised continued government control and better management of economic life. Ohlin quipped: "Can we be sure that controllers can understand and command [crisis] difficulties better than business leaders? Of course not!" Experience from the depression showed that a rational monetary policy in combination with countercyclical fiscal policy could stabilize the economy. He consequently pleaded for "an energetic, realistic business cycle policy without detrimental bureaucratic interventions in the management of individual enterprises".[197]

In October 1936, Cassel commented upon a discussion on economic planning which had taken place at a meeting organized by the Nordic Chamber of Commerce:

> The infatuation with economic planning is of Marxist origin. It belongs of course to socialism's inherited dogma that the liberal social order is

---

[195]Ibid., 8, 10, 13, 15.

[196]Ibid., 17.

[197]B. Ohlin, "Socialdemokraterna och kriserna", *Stockholms-Tidningen*, September 17, 1936.

"anarchic" and must be replaced by a socialist one, which will arrange production systematically according to the consumers' needs. In reality socialism does not at all follow this program. It is, at least as much as any other party, focused on producer interests and prepared to make considerable and sometimes exorbitant sacrifices in order to satisfy producer interests.[198]

Furthermore, planning suffered from two crucial weaknesses: "Firstly, a central organ can never design a satisfactory plan for a nation's economy". Secondly, the state-planned economy is unable "to adapt to the continually-shifting conditions of economic life".

Marxism has never understood that the superior value of liberalism lies in its great adaptability. Liberalism wants to secure an orderly economy precisely by compelling free economic forces in mutual competition to adapt to the constant demands posed by a highly changing economy. This constant adaptation is of great social economic value, and it is a gross abuse of slogans when one claims that economic activity is "social" only when it is pursued by the state or put under its control.

Ohlin's Middle Way

In late 1936, one of the most important documents in the 1930s Swedish debate on economic planning saw the light of day: Bertil Ohlin's book on "Free or Directed Economy" (*Fri eller dirigerad ekonomi*). When today you look back at the development of Swedish society, it seems as if Ohlin's middle-way vision was very far-sighted. The book therefore deserves to be presented in some detail.

Ohlin began his analysis by stating that the recent debate on how to organize society had been lively but obscure because it had revolved around "economic planning", a concept with many meanings. He then stated four goals for economic and social policy which he figured most people could agree on: (1) Economic growth and raised standard of

---

[198]G. Cassel, "Planhushållning", *Svenska Dagbladet*, October 12, 1936.

living. (2) Improved conditions for the poor. (3) Increased economic security for people. (4) Preserved personal freedom. Next, a structural transformation was outlined, with increased scale of production and decreased mobility, and a parallel psychological one: "instead of the 19th century merchant mentality an engineer mentality is gaining ground".[199] Ohlin thus seems to agree with, among others, institutionalists like Veblen and Myrdal. Government interventions must be gradually adapted to these new and constantly changing conditions.

Ohlin's next steps were a critique of *laissez-faire* liberalism and socialism and a plea for social liberalism. He criticized *laissez-faire* liberalism for assuming the existence of a natural condition which could only be distorted by government action and for assuming that there was congruence between the private and the public interest. The old liberalism, by advocating passivity during crises, was paving the way for dictatorship. He quickly dismissed Marxism and focused on the Swedish Social Democrats, who in many cases had "no idea of what a socialist society will look like but are nonetheless convinced that it will be in every way more efficient and better than the present one".[200] He stressed the importance of price formation and the drawbacks of public monopolies. He noted that socialists could not do much about the fact that crises in Sweden are mostly imported. He warned that the public administration would be overworked, exposed to corruption, involved in interest group conflicts and that the Social Democrats assumed the existence of some kind of supermen able to direct the whole economy.

Moving on to social liberalism, Ohlin stated that government interventions in recent decades had not been arbitrary but adapted to the new circumstances. As a result of the crisis, they had, however, been rather improvised. "Public measures should quite simply be executed more according to a plan and be less contradictory".[201] Ohlin stressed the importance of private ownership, private initiatives and decentralization and he indicated three cases where government initiatives were

---

[199]B. Ohlin, *Fri eller dirigerad ekonomi* (Stockholm: Studieledningen för Folkpartiets Ungdomsförbund, 1936), 25–26.

[200]Ibid., 59.

[201]Ibid., 88.

important: (1) When economic benefits can be reaped in a distant future. (2) When benefits are indirect and scattered. (3) When monopoly is natural and competition uneconomic. His next step was to list six important government activities: (1) Social security. (2) Public enterprise. (3) Public control. (4) Framework planning. (5) Business cycle policy. (6) Economic policy for the longer run.

Since presently we are mainly concerned with economic planning, we will focus on points 4 and 6 on Ohlin's agenda. The "frame", according to Ohlin, consists of habits and legislation. The latter means "fixed rules of the game, which everyone must obey. The game can thus unfold with less friction and more efficiency".[202] Ohlin's concepts can readily be translated into Douglass North's terminology some 50 years later, where framework corresponds to institutions and friction to transaction costs. As examples of framework planning, Ohlin cited urban and regional planning, tariffs, agricultural regulation, measures to increase economic (not least labour) mobility, support for economic and technological research, monetary and fiscal countercyclical policies, study and spread of economic statistics. He also advocated an economic policy with a longer time horizon, and quoted extensively from a 1935 memorandum on social trends by Karin Kock and Tage Erlander (later Swedish Prime Minister for many years). Referring to a statement by Sir Josiah Stamp, he underlined the importance of cooperative research efforts in business and of stronger central labour market organizations. Ohlin thus seems to suggest much of what was to evolve in Sweden: regional planning, strong labour market organizations, measures to increase mobility in the labour market, business cycle research—the National Institute of Economic Research (*Konjunkturinstitutet*) had already been decided when he wrote his book—and long-term investigations.

However, Ohlin admitted, even a social liberal organization had its weak spots, mainly the risk of creating inflexibility and becoming dependent on powerful vested interests when intervening in the income distribution. Finally, he had something to say about freedom. He noted, as Myrdal had done the year before, that in the nineteenth-century liberal society, people were constrained not so much by state regulation as

---

[202]Ibid., 111.

by conventions and traditions, i.e. by informal constraints. Over time, a shift was taking place towards formal constraints.[203] He advocated balance between freedom and efficiency and noted the complex relation between freedom and security (where increased security may induce a feeling of freedom). Freedom of thought and expression must however not be limited, even if a dictatorship should prove able to offer larger material gains. "Freedom of thought may only be restricted at major crises in the lives of nations, and then only temporarily".[204]

Ohlin's book attracted considerable attention. Olof Wennås has surveyed a number of reviews in newspapers close to the Liberal Party. They were in general very appreciative. According to a Social Democratic newspaper, Ohlin's outlook could be labelled liberal socialism as well as social liberalism. In some quarters, however, the verdict was apparently harsher.[205] Lewin mentions a review in a journal published by the Federation of Swedish Industries in which several of Ohlin's positions were regarded almost as acts of "ideological treason".[206]

When Heckscher published a review of Ohlin's book, he remarked that *laissez-faire* "as described by Professor Ohlin has never existed anywhere or anytime and has presently no advocate even in the realm of thought". At the same time, he was relieved to find that Ohlin had not exposed "the kind of socialism under liberal flag which some of his friends and adversaries had expected, but rather an honest attempt to stake out his own path".[207]

Sven Brisman wrote a long and winding review of Ohlin's book, which he perceived as an expression of common sense. He had one

---

[203]Sweden of today is often portrayed as a "state individualist" society. The basic idea is that there is a strong interplay between government and individuals and that individuals have been "set free" from other collective affinities. One side of this phenomenon may be that formal rules have to a large extent replaced informal ones. As mentioned in a previous note, Heckscher in his 1934 "showdown" said that liberalism accepts individuals and state but not formations in between. Seen through Heckscher's glasses, Sweden of today is thus a liberal society.

[204]Ohlin, *Fri eller dirigerad ekonomi*, 223.

[205]Wennås, "Bertil Ohlin om socialismen".

[206]Lewin, *Planhushållningsdebatten*, 142.

[207]E. Heckscher, "En ekonomisk programskrift", *Dagens Nyheter*, December 23, 1936.

main objection. He could not accept that Ohlin had lumped together *laissez-faire* and classical liberalism. He had himself been an active Liberal, with a feeling of solidarity towards socialism and without fear of state intervention in economic life. There had, however, been a realignment in 1920, when communists took over in Russia and socialists in Sweden appeared with a communist programme. When economic planning "spread across the world like an epidemic", it was only natural if a liberal felt that it could be somewhat more useful to apply the brake and not the accelerator.[208]

Keynes in the Limelight

In 1936, Keynes' *General Theory* appeared, and since it is generally seen as having eclipsed many of the arguments for a more comprehensive economic planning, we will note the leading Swedish economists' basic reactions without going into theoretical detail.[209] Davidson was first among the older generation to react. In late 1936, he dealt with Keynes *General Theory* in three articles in *Ekonomisk Tidskrift*. He spent much energy defending his "lifetime hero" David Ricardo, but also attacked Keynes for mixing the solutions of two different problems, unemployment and income distribution, in a way which entailed "an extraordinary intervention by the state in the economy".[210]

An experiment of this kind has only been conducted in one country, namely Russia, but how this experiment has turned out nobody outside Russia can say with any degree of certainty. The prevailing opinion outside Russia seems to be that the experiment has turned out in a way which ought to be very forbidding.[211]

[208]S. Brisman, "Liberalismen och planhushållningen", *Göteborgs Handels- och Sjöfartstidning*, February 5, 1937.

[209]The book was eventually (1942) translated into Swedish by Leif Björk and Tord Palander.

[210]D. Davidson, "Nationalekonomien i stöpsleven: Tredje artikeln", *Ekonomisk Tidskrift* 38(5–6) (1936): 104.

[211]Ibid. At the end of the article, Davidson modified this statement by saying that the experiment had perhaps also been conducted in Hitler's Germany and Mussolini's Italy.

David Davidson noted that Lionel Robbins and Ludwig von Mises had disputed the idea of a planned economy and added that "Sweden's workers would certainly not be willing to submit to such a regime". Unemployment could preferably be remedied by "the Swedish method"—"to give *real* work to all workers [...] during the *whole* time span of the crisis, but *only* during this time"—leaving the structure and organization of society intact. The Swedish experiment was "a fully effective way of combatting unemployment" and Davidson therefore called for an account of the Swedish method in English, French and German to make it known outside Sweden.[212]

Cassel and Keynes had been attuned in the 1920s in their criticism of the demands made on Germany for reparations, they had met at high-level conferences in the 1920s and early 1930s, they had corresponded in an amicable way about their books and articles, and Cassel had been behind Keynes' election to the Royal Swedish Academy of Sciences in 1924. However, Cassel's reactions to *General Theory* in a series of articles in 1937 was one of repugnance: "Among the numerous products of the slump which still haunts us, Keynes' attempt at a complete revolution in economic science occupies a position of special eminence in terms of its vastly harmful effects".[213] Cassel's primary objection to Keynes' theory was that it was not general. It was based on the artificial conditions prevailing in the British economy during the depression and failed to reflect crucial features of a normal economy:

> One such feature is undoubtedly progress, and even the most elementary picture of society must explain in broad outline how progress comes about. This aspect of the economy disappears in a most disquieting manner in the picture of a society falling into hopeless stagnation. However, since this stagnation seems to be mainly the result of temporary government measures, it is impossible to see in it a necessity conditioned by given economic factors.[214]

---

[212]Ibid., 105, 107, 122.
[213]G. Cassel, "En förvänd samhällsbild", *Sunt Förnuft* 17(May) (1937): 137.
[214]Ibid.

Cassel scrutinized Keynes' theory in articles directed to an international audience and concluded that there was no defect in the capitalist mechanism that would cause permanent unemployment. There is always an equilibrium solution that ensures full employment for all factors of production. Unemployment is caused by temporary disturbances and adjustment. The problem during the slump of the 1930s had been inadequate investment, not excessive saving. This was the consequence of incorrect monetary policy, capricious state intervention and confiscatory taxation.[215] In an editorial, Cassel concluded that Keynes was exerting "a soaring and confusing influence". "He [...] joins the long line of failed prophets, who, during previous stages of development, have claimed that technical progress has come to an end".[216]

Ohlin's celebrated "Notes" in the *Economic Journal* for 1937—in which the Stockholm School was presented to the world—met with Cassel's approval, precisely because of their dynamic element. Cassel wrote in a letter to Ohlin: "I have read with great interest your articles against Keynes in the Economic Journal. Without doubt, it is very valuable, in opposing Keynes, to present, as you do, a well-based dynamic theory".[217]

Heckscher was also concerned about Keynes' rising star. He had in 1924 written an appreciative entry on Keynes for a Swedish encyclopaedia[218] and he had corresponded with Keynes, not least in the latter's role as editor of *Economic Journal*. In a new entry, Heckscher wrote that Keynes had "associated himself with mercantilist interpretations" and introduced a new terminology which

---

[215]G. Cassel, "The Equilibrium of the Capital Market", *Skandinaviska Kreditaktiebolaget Quarterly Review* 18(3) (July) (1937): 41–44 and "Keynes' 'General Theory'", *International Labour Review* 36(4) (October) (1937).

[216]G. Cassel, "Skall kapitalräntan försvinna?" *Svenska Dagbladet*, August 4, 1937. In spite of Cassel's condemnation, Keynes was generous in his verdict at Cassel's death: "he was perhaps the last of the great economists of the older generation. We all studied his works. We grew up with them, as it were. [...] His integrity, energy and character is respected by economists all over the world". See Svenska Dagbladet, "Gustav Cassels livsgärning", *Svenska Dagbladet*, January 17, 1945.

[217]Letter from Cassel to Ohlin, July 15, 1937.

[218]E. Heckscher, "Keynes, John Maynard", *Nordisk Familjebok* (1924).

often caused misunderstandings.[219] Keynes had written in a letter that he intended to use Heckscher's *Mercantilism* "to write a chapter in my new book upon the relation between Mercantilist theory and current ideas".[220] Heckscher was not amused by the result. As his colleague Arthur Montgomery said, he seems to have felt that Keynes had read *Mercantilism* in the same way as the devil reads the Bible.[221]

When referring to the *General Theory*, Heckscher called Keynes a stimulating and useful author, but he could not understand why Keynes was chosen as a "practical leader" now that the business cycle theory was completely confused.[222] Heckscher's real showdown with Keynes, however, did not come until a decade later when he drew the same conclusion as Cassel before him: Keynes' *General Theory* was not general but was the fruit of large-scale fixed capital formation and of the Great Depression. Its "real impulse has come from the never-ending unemployment of the interwar era, by which he almost seems to have been obsessed. Never before, perhaps, has a work laying claims to universal validity been based to such a degree upon a single point of view".[223]

Ohlin, as mentioned, reacted upon the appearance of the *General Theory* with two articles" in the *Economic Journal*. The story of his "Notes" has been told many times and concerns theoretical issues of no interest in the present context. Suffice to say that Ohlin wished to start "a discussion of two independent attacks on the same set of problems", i.e. the attacks by Swedish/Stockholm economists, inspired by Knut Wicksell, and those by Keynes.[224]

[219]E. Heckscher, "Keynes, J.M.", *Nordisk Familjebok* (1936).

[220]Letter from Keynes to Heckscher, May 15, 1935.

[221]*Tre tal hållna vid den middag som ett antal kolleger och lärjungar gav för Eli F. Heckscher och hans anhöriga den 13 december 1944 på restaurangen Tre Kronor i Stockholm* (Stockholm, 1945).

[222]E. Heckscher, "Inför konjunkturläget", *Dagens Nyheter*, January 23, 1937.

[223]E. Heckscher, "Något om Keynes 'General Theory' ur ekonomisk-historisk synpunkt", *Ekonomisk Tidskrift* 48(3) (1946): 181.

[224]B. Ohlin, "Some Notes on the Stockholm Theory of Savings and Investment I", *Economic Journal* 47(185) (1937): 53.

Automatic Expansion

The committees of inquiry into unemployment, various trades, commercial, currency and credit policy, and the trend of economic activity, had by 1936 reached the point where "the measures were ripening more palpably into a preliminary stage of modern planning".[225] A number of committees, however, simply got nowhere. This was the case, for example, with the committees on coffee and oil monopolies, the insurance industry, monopoly control and state assistance to rationalization of business and industry. In other areas, they were more successful. The National Institute of Economic Research (*Konjunkturinstitutet*) was founded in 1937, and, in 1938, a decision was taken to introduce tax-free investment funds to be activated in periods of depression.

Bagge, in a political speech in the autumn of 1937, portrayed the "millenniums" Russia, Germany, and Italy. Freedoms of thought and expression were eliminated, economy and labour market were controlled by politicians, and autarchy and nationalism were at the forefront. He concluded that "all economic planning must finally be more and more focused on the consumers' right to use his income – the regulator which ultimately guides the so called private capitalist society". The Nordic countries, however, fortunately lacked the kind of mass mentality or "*serf mentality*" which was a precondition for this kind of dictatorships.[226] In this matter, Bagge referred to a book by Carl Joachim Hambro, a Norwegian conservative politician.[227]

According to Cassel, people joined the movement of government expansion just as ladies compete in the latest fashion regarding short or long dresses. There was also a confusion of society and state and people imagined that nationalization was the same as pursuing the interest of society. Such a misunderstanding would evaporate if people would only realize that the production of bikes and cars had done more for the well-being of the citizens than any government intervention in the

---

[225]K. Wickman, *Makroekonomisk planering – orsaker och utveckling* (Uppsala: Almqvist & Wiksell International, 1980), 70.

[226]G. Bagge, *Politiska tal år 1937* (Stockholm, 1937), 9–10.

[227]C. J. Hambro, *Moderne mentalitet* (Oslo: Gyldendal, 1937).

economy. Government had important missions to fulfil, not least the management of the monetary system. However, every new expansion meant new claims upon government. "An increasing overstrain of state organs, particularly government and Riksdag, is already evident for everybody".[228]

> This expansion has to a large extent become automatic. When protection or subsidies are granted in one area, there will be a demand for corresponding or compensating measures in other areas. [...] In their struggle over trade, states find ever new reasons for intervention in the economy. One people must protect itself from aggressive actions from another people. And so on in cumulative interaction.

In this kind of struggle, dictatorships had the upper hand. For those who wished to protect personal freedom and responsibility, it was less important in what shape the dictatorship emerged, whether it was communism, fascism on Nazism. "For us in Sweden, it's all about fighting against any form of dictatorship in our own country, whatever shape it may take on". Cassel, however, saw tendencies towards dictatorship also in Sweden as the government pushed through its proposals, allowing little time or space for discussion in the parliament, the public administration and the media.[229]

At an Economic Society meeting in 1938, Myrdal unveiled his ideas about the future of Swedish agricultural policy[230] and, in a way, admitted that Heckscher had been right when talking of planning without a plan:

> One intervention was added to the other, and eventually we had a system of agricultural regulation whereby practically all agricultural products had gotten their markets regulated and screened off from abroad. Typical of

---

[228]G. Cassel, "Statsmaktens Expansion", *Svenska Dagbladet*, September 11, 1937.

[229]G. Cassel, "På väg till envälde", *Svenska Dagbladet*, June 8, 1938.

[230]Myrdal's presentation was a summary of a book he had just completed; the preface written in February. G. Myrdal, *Jordbrukspolitiken under omläggning* (Stockholm: Kooperativa Förbundets Bokförlag, 1938).

all these interventions [...] is that the measures neither individually nor in total were intended as a long-term agricultural policy.[231]

No plan of this system had "ever existed on paper or in anybody's brain", but it was anyway part of the general crisis policy and intended to protect the agricultural population from ruin. During the crisis, prices had been regulated and surpluses been dumped abroad. Now that the crisis was over, the question was "how a more planned agricultural policy for the long run can be designed". Myrdal started out by presenting three premises: The living standard of the agricultural population must be protected. This requires government involvement. And for the next ten years, there would hardly be any reduction of the agricultural population, the solution "which played such a prominent role in the old liberal economy". He then examined three hardly passable ways of attaining balance between supply and demand. Limitation of production would meet resistance from the farmers. Dumping could not be applied in the long run. Increased domestic consumption could be attained through rationalization, lower production costs and lower prices but would hardly suffice to raise farmer's incomes. The solution, according to Myrdal, was to replace price support with production cost support. This might seem as a peculiar way of solving a problem of overproduction, but would work if prices were simultaneously lowered so that consumption increased. One possible advantage was that the cost would be visible in the government budget. Myrdal, however, dismissed the idea of transparency as "the old liberal attitude"; it was better to hand out support in "a more covert way".[232]

Ohlin glanced towards Germany where state activity (armament) consumed ever more resources. "One must admit that in Germany during a short period of time a real socialization of society has been accomplished", he wrote and continued: "For sure, the non-orthodox Social Democracy, in e.g. Sweden, could learn much from a study of German experiences".[233] Was this perhaps a warning that pragmatic Social Democrats should beware of forceful state intervention?

---

[231]Nationalekonomiska Föreningen, "Jordbrukspolitikens svårigheter", March 3, 1938, 59.

[232]Ibid., 59, 63–64, 72.

[233]B. Ohlin, "Ekonomi och politik", *Stockholms-Tidningen*, September 18, 1938.

When Marquis Childs, author of *Sweden, the Middle Way*, a book which had received much attention, in 1938 published a new book, *This is Democracy*, Ohlin elaborated on it fairly extensively. Childs had been surprised to find that Sweden had so many labour market conflicts and Ohlin pointed out that conflicts in the construction industry in 1933–1934 had upset the government's economic policy. Economic planning would be impossible if there was a risk of further such events.[234]

After Wigforss had made a speech in Gothenburg on the issue of cooperation between state and business life, Ohlin wrote an editorial in a very cooperative spirit:

> A basically free economy can surely not be defended by rejecting new currents and letting the organization cling to the old. It is vital to find such forms of cooperation, not only between enterprises but also between the business community and the government, that the demands of our time are met without the dynamic force of a free economy being lost. Thereby the danger of socialization measures and far-reaching government control is reduced.[235]

When Gunnar Westin Silverstolpe in 1938 published an economic history of the period 1880–1930, he devoted some space to Soviet style planning as it had been displayed by Sidney and Betarice Webb. His own comment was that both the invisible hand of Adam Smith and "the fully visible hand directing a centralized planned economy" were imperfect. The combination of Soviet planning and world economic depression had placed economic planning on the agenda also in the Western world under the heading "Above all, try something". The idea that "whatever the government does is according to plan" grew into to the perception that the government can direct a national economy in order to use available resources more efficiently. However, it had not

---

[234]B. Ohlin, "Är detta demokrati?", *Stockholms-Tidningen*, October 26, 1938 and "Hur går det om …? Några demokratiska grundproblem apropå Marquis W. Childs nya Sverigebok", *Stockholms-Tidningen*, October 28, 1938.

[235]B. Ohlin, "Hr Wigforss och näringslivet", *Stockholms-Tidningen*, November 6, 1938.

gone so far "that people's efforts to manage on their own and take their own initiatives were criminalized".[236]

We Are All Planners Now!

In early 1939, Erik Lundberg, head of the National Institute of Economic Research from its start in 1937,[237] opened a discussion of the prospects of economic policy based on recent experiences in other countries. Lundberg wished to discuss what to do in case of another depression and not in a war situation. He saw the lack of confidence between governments and the business community as a reason for the rather failed experiments of the New Deal in America and the Popular Front in France. Germany had taken "the full step into a centrally controlled and directed government investment activity".[238] However, as Lundberg did not wish to discuss a war economy, he found this example less interesting. In comparison with these cases, Sweden's economic policy had been comparably well balanced. Heckscher, in turn, was disappointed that Lundberg focused on business cycle policy and looked upon the prospect of war as a disturbance of planned economic activity. For Heckscher, preparations for a possible war were at the top of the agenda. Ohlin could not refrain from expressing his joy that his older colleagues were losing steam and asked if they had not yet modified their ideas "in accordance with the new thoughts, which according to the scientific literature have an overwhelming majority of followers".[239] Arthur Montgomery viewed business cycle policy and war economy as intertwined under the prevailing circumstances.

---

[236]G. Westin Silverstolpe, *Välstånd och fattigdom*, in *Vår egen tids historia 1880–1930*, vol. 5, ed. Y. Lorents (Stockholm: Bonniers, 1938), 307, 603–604, 607.

[237]See R. G. H. Henriksson (ed.), *Konjunkturinstitutet under Erik Lundbergs tid: Tillbakablickar vid 50-årsjubiléet* (Stockholm: Konjunkturinstitutet, 1987).

[238]Nationalekonomiska Föreningen, "Den ekonomiska politikens möjligheter", April 25, 1939, 66.

[239]Ibid., 80.

Myrdal, for his part, presented the Swedish success story to the American public in a Bronson Cutting Memorial lecture in Washington, published in *Survey Graphic*. As Sweden found itself in the shadow of totalitarian dictatorships, Soviet Russia and Nazi Germany, it had to manage its democracy efficiently. "Failure to make our system work efficiently would mean for us succumbing to the pressure of the two totalitarian ideologies, the red and the brown", Myrdal noted. He continued by stating that "we are prepared to face our problems squarely: we investigate our shortcomings intensively, and use the technique of social engineering to plan for their removal". Some of the measures employed to handle the depression had been improvised, but Sweden was now well prepared to face another crisis: "The aim is, not to be caught unawares by the next crisis, to have the blueprint at hand, the advance decisions made, so the government need only press the button to set the necessary machinery in motion".[240] Furthermore, the Swedish business and finance sector was not afraid of the socialist government, which was to a great extent

> due to the policy of the Social-Democrats which has not been unfriendly to business. The Swedish socialists have shown themselves fully aware of the necessity for keeping up production in order to reach their goals. Increase in public control over production by means other than socialization has been very much in the interests of maintaining and stabilizing production.[241]

Confronted with the prospect of war, Cassel and Heckscher all of a sudden stood out as the prime advocates of economic planning! Cassel predicted that government interventions in case of war would expose the economy to a "violent shock". It was thus of utmost importance that the Swedish government designed a coherent programme, a "master plan", for the transition from a peace to a war economy and that

---

[240]G. Myrdal, *Maintaining Democracy in Sweden*. Two articles by Gunnar Myrdal. (I) With dictators as neighbors; (II) The defenses of democracy (Reprinted from Survey Graphic and Distributed by Albert Bonnier Publishing House, New York, 1939), 3, 6.

[241]Ibid., 13.

thereby the public expenditure on unemployment, construction, agriculture, etc. was reduced, as the expenses for defence increased.[242]

At the next meeting of the Economic Society, in May 1939, Heckscher declared that he agreed with Cassel with respect to "the desirability of assembling all the various ingredients of the immense task of defensive economic preparedness into a comprehensive plan", adding that economic planning "in the literal sense faces its greatest task in a war situation".[243]

Ohlin still, less than four months before the outbreak of World War II, figured that Heckscher's demands were somewhat exaggerated. However, measures had to be taken as a preparation for mobilization. He referred to all the government commissions involved in these preparations. Heckscher had warned that inflation would be inevitable. Ohlin argued that a shortage of certain goods would arise but that this was something very different from a general inflationary pressure. If wages could be held constant, major price increases could be avoided on the condition that there was "*government control of all private investments*".[244]

After the outbreak of the war, Heckscher concluded that his "blackening" at the May meeting had been surpassed by reality and he demanded "proper planning" of how "an isolated Sweden can cope".[245] Ohlin retorted that Heckscher's feeling of having been seen as someone "painting things in black" was a misunderstanding.[246] The two continued their ill-tempered discussion. The next day, Heckscher wrote to Ohlin that the two were sliding into the same kind of relation as had prevailed between Wicksell and Cassel and that they should therefore not appear together in public debates. Ohlin concurred.[247]

---

[242]G. Cassel, "Generalplan efterlyses", *Svenska Dagbladet*, May 11, 1939.

[243]Nationalekonomiska Föreningen, "Sveriges ekonomi inför världsläget", May 16, 1939, 103, 115.

[244]B. Ohlin, "Mobiliserings- och krigsekonomi", *Stockholms-Tidningen*, May 17, 1939.

[245]Nationalekonomiska Föreningen, "Den aktuella pris- och lönepolitikens möjligheter", October 5, 1939, 161.

[246]Ibid., 174.

[247]Letter from Heckscher to Ohlin October 6 and from Ohlin to Heckscher October 9, 1939.

Cassel, as Heckscher, contended that the government had not been able to produce a coherent programme. He complained about the creation of a "credit board", with the mission to achieve "a central planning of the credit market", which he regarded as a step on the road towards dictatorship, and about government confusion and chaos. "Where is, behind of all this, a guiding hand?"[248]

The world war enforced a tough regulation of the economy. All shades of political opinion had to ride out the storm together. There was no room for debates about economic planning—and no great reason either, since the planning enforced by the war was considered to be a temporary phenomenon. Nevertheless, Cassel was worried that state direction, which would be necessary in the transition from a war to a peace economy, might become permanent.[249]

The war in a sense meant that a massive experiment in economic planning took place in an atmosphere of tolerably political unity. "It is clear that planning practice advanced in comparison to the 1930s", writes Wickman.[250] In the 1930s, the main task had been to pull the economy out of the depression. During the war, it was to strengthen defence while simultaneously keeping the economy in balance.

References

20:de svenska handelskammarmötet i Borås den 18 och 19 juni 1934: Protokoll och handlingar. Stockholm: K.L. Beckmans Boktryckeri, 1934.

Åkerman, J. Ekonomiskt framåtskridande och ekonomiska kriser. Stockholm: Kooperativa Förbundets Bokförlag, 1931.

Åkerman, J. Some Lessons of the World Depression. Stockholm: Nordiska Bokhandeln, 1931.

Åkerman, J. Economic Progress and Economic Crises. London: Macmillan, 1932.

Åkerman, J. "Planhushållning och tidshushållning". Ekonomiska Samfundets Tidskrift 24 (1932): 1–9.

---

[248]G. Cassel, "Planlöshet och förmynderskap", Svenska Dagbladet, November 19, 1939.

[249]G. Cassel, "Stat och näringsliv: En framtidsblick", Sunt Förnuft 22(December) (1942).

[250]Wickman, Makroekonomisk planering, 77.

Andreen, P. G. *Gösta Bagge som samhällsbyggare: Kommunalpolitiker – Socialpolitiker – Ecklesiastikminister*. Stockholm: Almqvist & Wiksell International, 1999.

Arg. "Cassel viser oss den enkle vei ut av krisen og vanviddet: Fast prisnivå, faste valutakurser". *Aftenposten*, October 5, 1934.

Aronson, T. *Gösta Bagges politiska tänkande: En studie i 1900-talets svenska konservatism*. Stockholm: Norstedts Juridik, 1993.

Bagge, G. *Svensk konservatism och tidslägets krav: Fyra föredrag*. Södertälje: Axlings Bok- och Tidskriftstryckeri, 1934.

Bagge, G. *Politiska tal år 1937*. Stockholm, 1937.

Betänkande om folkförsörjning och arbetsfred, part I–II. Stockholm: Isaac Marcus Boktryckeriaktiebolag, 1935 (SOU 1935: 65 and 66).

Brisman, S. "De unga nationalekonomernas revolt". *Göteborgs Handels- och Sjöfartstidning*, December 5, 1930.

Brisman, S. "Ekonomiska småskrifter". *Göteborgs Handels- och Sjöfartstidning*, April 24, 1934.

Brisman, S. "Liberalismen och planhushållningen". *Göteborgs Handels- och Sjöfartstidning*, February 5, 1937.

Carlström, O. "Planhushållning och diktatur". *Svenska Dagbladet*, March 4, 1934.

Cassel, G. "Hvad är socialism?" *Svenska Dagbladet*, October 20, 1910.

Cassel, G. *The Theory of Social Economy*. London: T. Fisher Unwin, 1923.

Cassel, G. "Dogmatik och verklighet". *Svenska Dagbladet*, February 26, 1926.

Cassel, G. "Vår tids största charlataneri". *Svenska Dagbladet*, December 5, 1926.

Cassel, G. *Socialism eller framåtskridande*. Stockholm: P. A. Norstedt & Söners Förlag, 1928.

Cassel, G. "Lloyd Georges valprogram". *Svenska Dagbladet*, April 10, 1929.

Cassel, G. "Statsmakt på avvägar". *Svenska Dagbladet*, December 31, 1929.

Cassel, G. "Kapitalistsamhället". *Svenska Dagbladet*, May 3, 1931.

Cassel, G. "Överproduktion". *Svenska Dagbladet*, June 17, 1931.

Cassel, G. "Understödspolitikens kris". *Svenska Dagbladet*, August 19, 1931.

Cassel, G. "Överproduktion, planhushållning". *Svenska Dagbladet*, April 2, 1933.

Cassel, G. "Bristande planhushållning". *Svenska Dagbladet*, April 7, 1933.

Cassel, G. "Roosevelts Experiment". *Svenska Dagbladet*, August 23, 1933.

Cassel, G. "Staten och näringslivet". *Sunt Förnuft* 13(December) (1933): 397–399.

Cassel, G. "Roosevelt som reformator". *Svenska Dagbladet*, December 23, 1933.

Cassel, G. "Meningslös förödelse". *Svenska Dagbladet*, December 31, 1933.

Cassel, G. "Planhushållning och diktatur". *Svenska Dagbladet*, February 25, 1934.

Cassel, G. "Planekonomiens villfarelser". *Svenska Dagbladet*, March 3, 1934.

Cassel, G. "Professor Cassel preciserar sin uppfattning". *Svenska Dagbladet*, March 4, 1934.

Cassel, G. *"Planhushållning" Diskussion med inledningsföredrag av professor Gustav Cassel vid Sveriges Industriförbunds årsmöte den 17 April 1934*, no. 2. Stockholm, 1934.

Cassel, G. "From Protectionism Through Planned Economy to Dictatorship". *International Conciliation*. Documents for the year 1934. New York (1934): 307–325.

Cassel, G. "Planned Economy". *American Bankers Association Journal* 26(July) (1934): 15–17, 49.

Cassel, G. "Arbetslöshet och kolonisation". *Svenska Dagbladet*, September 20, 1934.

Cassel, G. "Socialismens misstag". *Svenska Dagbladet*, November 10, 1934.

Cassel, G. "Sverige och diktaturerna". *Svenska Dagbladet*, November 14, 1934.

Cassel, G. "Vårt folks livsfråga". *Svenska Dagbladet*, November 25, 1934.

Cassel, G. "Samhällsintresset i befolkningsfrågan". *Svenska Dagbladet*, November 27, 1934.

Cassel, G. "Svar till Myrdals". *Svenska Dagbladet*, December 9, 1934.

Cassel, G. *Liv eller död*. Stockholm: Albert Bonniers Förlag, 1935.

Cassel, G. "Statsingripandets rationalisering". *Svenska Dagbladet*, February 10, 1935.

Cassel, G. "Borgerlighetens prövostund". *Svenska Dagbladet*, February 22, 1935.

Cassel, G. "Folkrepresentation och planhushållning". *Svenska Dagbladet*, March 8, 1935.

Cassel, G. "En centralekonomisk utredning". *Svenska Dagbladet*, March 13, 1935.

Cassel, G. "Planlös jordbrukspolitik". *Sunt Förnuft* 15(March) (1935): 57–58.

Cassel, G. "Hushållning". *Sunt Förnuft* 15(May) (1935): 131–132.

Cassel, G. "Andlig frihet och ekonomisk". *Svenska Dagbladet*, August 25, 1935.

Cassel, G. "Samhälleliga värden". *Sunt Förnuft* 15(Christmas) (1935): 403–404.

Cassel, G. "Ryssland som mönster!" *Svenska Dagbladet*, April 25, 1936.

Cassel, G. *Stat och näringsliv: Föredrag vid Hakonbolagets årsstämma 25 maj 1936*. Västerås: Hakonbolaget, 1936.

Cassel, G. "Planhushållning". *Svenska Dagbladet*, October 12, 1936.

Cassel, G. "En förvänd samhällsbild". *Sunt Förnuft* 17(May) (1937): 137–139.

Cassel, G. "The Equilibrium of the Capital Market". *Skandinaviska Kreditaktiebolaget Quarterly Review* 18(3) (July) (1937): 41–44.

Cassel, G. "Skall kapitalräntan försvinna?" *Svenska Dagbladet*, August 4, 1937.

Cassel, G. "Statsmaktens Expansion". *Svenska Dagbladet*, September 11, 1937.

Cassel, G. "Keynes' 'General Theory'". *International Labour Review* 36(4) (October) (1937): 437–445.

Cassel, G. "På väg till envälde". *Svenska Dagbladet*, June 8, 1938.

Cassel, G. "Generalplan efterlyses". *Svenska Dagbladet*, May 11, 1939.

Cassel, G. "Planlöshet och förmynderskap". *Svenska Dagbladet*, November 19, 1939.

Cassel, G. *I förnuftets tjänst*. Vol. 2. Stockholm: Natur och Kultur, 1941.

Cassel, G. "Stat och näringsliv: En framtidsblick". *Sunt Förnuft* 22(December) (1942): 305–307.

Dagens Nyheter. "Fallet Cassel". *Dagens Nyheter*, February 18, 1930.

Dagens Nyheter. "Gunnar Myrdal intog sin post med idéprogram". *Dagens Nyheter*, March 2, 1934.

Dagens Nyheter. "Planhushållning förkastas av industrin". *Dagens Nyheter*, April 18, 1934.

Dagens Nyheter. "Konjunkturen konfronterad med politiken. Planhushållningens troende och tvivlare i debatt". *Dagens Nyheter*, May 12, 1934.

Dagens Nyheter. "Demokratins framtid". *Dagens Nyheter*, January 7, 1935.

Dagens Nyheter. "Sysselsättningsfrågan dryftas på Arosmässan. Liberal planhushållning skulle göra susen, menar professor Ohlin". *Dagens Nyheter*, November 3, 1935.

Davidson, D. "Nationalekonomien i stöpsleven: Tredje artikeln". *Ekonomisk Tidskrift* 38(5–6) (1936): 103–124.

Euler, R. von, and J. Hagberg. "Leif Björk". *Dagens Nyheter*, July 4, 2000.

Forhandlinger ved det tiende nordiske nasjonaløkonomiske møte i Oslo den 17–19 juni 1935. "Kritisk vurdering av planøkonomien", 11–78. Oslo: Grøndahl & Søns Boktrykkeri, 1935.

Hambro, C. J. *Moderne mentalitet*. Oslo: Gyldendal, 1937.

Heckscher, E. "Keynes, John Maynard". *Nordisk Familjebok* (1924).

Heckscher, E. "Intryck från Ryssland I: Petersburg och Moskva". *Dagens Nyheter*, September 21, 1925.

Heckscher, E. "Intryck från Ryssland VI: 'Planhushållning' och förnöjsamhet". *Dagens Nyheter*, October 9, 1925.

Heckscher, E. "Inledande översikt". In *Bidrag till Sveriges ekonomiska och sociala historia under och efter världskriget*, edited by E. Heckscher, 3–40. Stockholm: P. A. Norstedt & Söner, 1926.

Heckscher, E. "Den icke-socialistiska framtidsstaten". *Dagens Nyheter*, February 17, 1928.

Heckscher, E. "Arbetslöshet och allmänna arbeten". *Dagens Nyheter*, March 26, 1929.

Heckscher, E. "General Survey". In *Sweden, Norway, Denmark and Iceland in the World War*, edited by E. Heckscher, K. Bergendahl, Wilhelm Keilhau, Einar Cohn, and Thorsteinn Thorsteinnson, 3–39. New Haven: Yale University Press, 1930.

Heckscher, E. "Planhushållning". *Dagens Nyheter*, March 1, 1930.

Heckscher, E. "Inmalningstvånget och dess konsekvenser". *Dagens Nyheter*, May 28, 1930.

Heckscher, E. "Striden om jordbruket". *Svensk Tidskrift* 29 (1930): 1–20.

Heckscher, E. "Liberalism, fascism, bolsjevism som ekonomiska system". *Svensk Tidskrift* 29 (1930): 519–541.

Heckscher, E. "Diktatur och teknik". *Dagens Nyheter*, March 22, 1933.

Heckscher, E. "Försvaret mot omstörtningen". *Dagens Nyheter*, March 29, 1933.

Heckscher, E. "Planned Economy Past and Present". *Index*, månadsskrift utgiven av Svenska Handelsbanken IX(5) (1934): 91–105.

Heckscher, E. *Tvångshushållning och "planhushållning"*. Stockholm: Kooperativa Förbundets Bokförlag, 1934.

Heckscher, E. "Det privata näringslivet i tvångshushållningens tid". *Föredrag hållna inför svenska ekonomföreningen*, no. 1. Stockholm, 1936.

Heckscher, E. "En ekonomisk programskrift". *Dagens Nyheter*, December 23, 1936.

Heckscher, E. "Keynes, J.M.". *Nordisk Familjebok* (1936).

Heckscher, E. "Inför konjunkturläget". *Dagens Nyheter*, January 23, 1937.

Heckscher, E. "Något om Keynes 'General Theory' ur ekonomisk-historisk synpunkt". *Ekonomisk Tidskrift* 48(3) (1946): 161–183.

Heckscher, E., and E. Heckscher. "Befolkningsfrågan som murbräcka". *Dagens Nyheter*, December 5, 1934.

Heckscher, E., and E. Heckscher. "Familjen i stöpsleven". *Dagens Nyheter*, December 7, 1934.

Henriksson, R. G. H. (ed.). *Konjunkturinstitutet under Erik Lundbergs tid: Tillbakablickar vid 50-årsjubiléet*. Stockholm: Konjunkturinstitutet, 1987.

Henriksson, R. G. H. "The Political Economy Club and the Stockholm School". In *The Stockholm School of Economics Revisited*, edited by L. Jonung, 41–74. Cambridge: Cambridge University Press, 1991.

Hirsch, A. *Minnen som dröjt kvar*. Stockholm: Lars Hökerbergs Bokförlag, 1953.

I-n, A. "Ryska bondsöner läsa i brigader, läraren konsult". *Dagens Nyheter*, October 4, 1931.

Kock, K. *Roosevelts program ur konjunktursynpunkt*. Stockholm: Kooperativa förbundets bokförlag, 1934.

Larsson, S.-E. *Bertil Ohlin*. Stockholm: Atlantis, 1998.

Lewin, L. *Planhushållningsdebatten*. Stockholm: Almqvist & Wiksell, 1967.

Lgr., A. "Ekonomisk veckorevy". *Dagens Nyheter*, January 14, 1934.

Lindahl, E. "Arbetslöshet och finanspolitik". *Ekonomisk Tidskrift* 37(1–2) (1935): 1–36.

Lindman, A. *Vår svenska väg: Urval av tal i 1934 års valrörelse*. Ulricehamn, 1934.

Lundberg, E. *Kriserna och ekonomerna*. Malmö: LiberFörlag, 1984.

Myrdal, G. *Vetenskap och politik i nationalekonomien*. Stockholm: Norstedt, 1930.

Myrdal, G. "Kring den praktiska nationalekonomiens problematik". *Ekonomisk Tidskrift* 33(2) (1931): 41–81.

Myrdal, G. "Socialpolitikens dilemma II". *Spektrum* 2(4) (1932): 13–31.

Myrdal, G. *Konjunktur och offentlig hushållning: En utredning*. Stockholm: Kooperativa förbundets bokförlag, 1933.

Myrdal, G. *Finanspolitikens ekonomiska verkningar*. Annex 5 to Arbetslöshetsutredningens betänkande II. Stockholm: Kungl. Boktryckeriet/ P. A. Norstedt & Söner, 1934 (SOU 1934:1).

Myrdal, G. "Installationsföreläsning den 31 mars 1934". In *Samhällskrisen och socialvetenskaperna*, 7–41. Stockholm: Kooperativa förbundets bokförlag, 1935.

Myrdal, G. *Jordbrukspolitiken under omläggning*. Stockholm: Kooperativa Förbundets Bokförlag, 1938.

Myrdal, G. *Maintaining Democracy in Sweden*. Two articles by Gunnar Myrdal. I. With Dictators as Neigbors; II. The Defenses of Democracy. Reprinted from Survey Graphic and Distributed by Albert Bonnier Publishing House, New York, 1939.

Myrdal, G. *The Political Element in the Development of Economic Theory*. London: Routledge & Kegan Paul, 1953.

Myrdal, A., and G. Myrdal. *Kris i befolkningsfrågan*. Stockholm: Bonnier, 1934.

Myrdal, A., and G. Myrdal. "Avfolkning eller samhällsreform". *Svenska Dagbladet*, December 6, 1934.

Nationalekonomiska Föreningen. "Inmalningen och vår spannmålspolitik", March 23, 1931.

Nationalekonomiska Föreningen. "Arbetslösheten och dess behandling", October 12, 1931.

Nationalekonomiska Föreningen. "Offentliga arbeten i depressionstider", November 25, 1932.

Nationalekonomiska Föreningen. "Arbetslöshetspolitiken", April 28, 1933.

Nationalekonomiska Föreningen. "Roosevelts rekonstruktionsprogram ur konjunktursynpunkt", January 22, 1934.

Nationalekonomiska Föreningen. "Aktuell arbetslöshet och arbetslöshetspolitik", April 27, 1934.

Nationalekonomiska Föreningen. "Planhushållning", November 20, 1934.

Nationalekonomiska Föreningen. "Statsstödet åt jordbruket", February 28, 1935.

Nationalekonomiska Föreningen. "Government Expenditure and Economic Activity", March 23, 1936.

Nationalekonomiska Föreningen. "Statens regulering av näringslivet", May 4, 1936.

Nationalekonomiska Föreningen. "Jordbrukspolitikens svårigheter", March 3, 1938.

Nationalekonomiska Föreningen. "Den ekonomiska politikens möjligheter", April 25, 1939.

Nationalekonomiska Föreningen. "Sveriges ekonomi inför världsläget", May 16, 1939.

Nationalekonomiska Föreningen. "Den aktuella pris- och lönepolitikens möjligheter", October 5, 1939.

New York Times. "Gustav Cassel's Warning". *New York Times*, January 17, 1945.

Nya Dagligt Allehanda. "En krigsförklaring". *Nya Dagligt Allehanda*, February 15, 1930.

Ohlin, B. "Den nyaste socialismen". *Stockholms-Tidningen*, April 26, 1925.

Ohlin, B. "Liberalismen vid skiljovägen". *Stockholms-Tidningen*, December 27, 1927.

Ohlin, B. "Liberalismen vid skiljovägen II". *Stockholms-Tidningen*, December 29, 1927.

Ohlin, B. "Den liberala framtidsstaten I". *Stockholms-Tidningen*, March 27, 1928.

Ohlin, B. "Den liberala framtidsstaten II". *Stockholms-Tidningen*, March 28, 1928.

Ohlin, B. "Lloyd George och arbetslösheten". *Stockholms-Tidningen*, April 18, 1929.

Ohlin, B. "Valet och arbetslösheten i England". *Stockholms-Tidningen*, May 26, 1929.

Ohlin, B. "Kris och planhushållning". *Stockholms-Tidningen*, July 12, 1932.

Ohlin, B. "Hur krisen botas". *Stockholms-Tidningen*, August 7, 1932.

Ohlin, B. "Planmässighetens krav". *Stockholms-Tidningen*, December 18, 1932.

Ohlin, B. "Väg ur depressionen: Keynes får instämmande från Times". *Stockholms-Tidningen*, April 2, 1933.

Ohlin, B. "Den fria världsmarknaden". *Stockholms-Tidningen*, May 16, 1933.

Ohlin, B. "Roosevelts ekonomiska politik". *Stockholms-Tidningen*, June 2, 1933.

Ohlin, B. "Amerikas experiment: Det är med prisstegring som med vin: verkan beror på kvantiteten". *Stockholms-Tidningen*, July 20, 1933.

Ohlin, B. "Ordnad revolution hellre än kommunistisk! Männen kring Amerikas nye president". *Stockholms-Tidningen*, July 30, 1933.

Ohlin, B. "Den revolutionära verkligheten". *Stockholms-Tidningen*, August 5, 1933.

Ohlin, B. "Organisation och anpassning". *Stockholms-Tidningen*, August 13, 1933.

Ohlin, B. "Roosevelts prövotid". *Stockholms-Tidningen*, August 20, 1933.

Ohlin, B. "Byggnadskonflikten". *Stockholms-Tidningen*, August 22, 1933.

Ohlin, B. "Ekonomi och demokrati". *Stockholms-Tidningen*, December 30, 1933.

Ohlin, B. "Diktaturernas uppkomst". *Stockholms-Tidningen*, April 4, 1934.

Ohlin, B. "Bör finanspolitiken omläggas?" *Stockholms-Tidningen*, April 26, 1934.

Ohlin, B. "Nya vindar i U.S.A.?" *Stockholms-Tidningen*, May 2, 1934.

Ohlin, B. "Budgeten och framtiden". *Stockholms-Tidningen*, June 16, 1934.

Ohlin, B. "Roosevelts industripolitik". *Stockholms-Tidningen*, July 19, 1934.

Ohlin, B. "En ny ekonomisk politik?" *Stockholms-Tidningen*, July 25, 1934.

Ohlin, B. "Socialism och krispolitik". *Stockholms-Tidningen*, August 26, 1934.

Ohlin, B. "Folkpartiet, liberalismen och framtiden". *Stockholms-Tidningen*, October 23, 1934.

Ohlin, B. "Hushållning och anpassning". *Stockholms-Tidningen*, November 22, 1934.

Ohlin, B. "Fronten mot statssocialismen". *Stockholms-Tidningen*, January 20, 1935.

Ohlin, B. "Lloyd George contra Chamberlain". *Stockholms-Tidningen*, July 31, 1935.

Ohlin, B. "En engelsk femårsplan utan partifärg". *Stockholms-Tidningen*, August 16, 1935.

Ohlin, B. "Mammututredningens dilemma". *Stockholms-Tidningen*, December 22, 1935.

Ohlin, B. "Krispolitik och socialism". *Stockholms-Tidningen*, January 19, 1936.

Ohlin, B. "Socialdemokraterna och kriserna". *Stockholms-Tidningen*, September 17, 1936.

Ohlin, B. *Fri eller dirigerad ekonomi*. Stockholm: Studieledningen för Folkpartiets Ungdomsförbund, 1936.

Ohlin, B. "Some Notes on the Stockholm Theory of Savings and Investment I". *Economic Journal* 47(185) (March) (1937): 53–69.

Ohlin, B. "Ekonomi och politik". *Stockholms-Tidningen*, September 18, 1938.

Ohlin, B. "Är detta demokrati?" *Stockholms-Tidningen*, October 26, 1938.

Ohlin, B. "Hur går det om …? Några demokratiska grundproblem apropå Marquis W. Childs nya Sverigebok". *Stockholms-Tidningen*, October 28, 1938.

Ohlin, B. "Hr Wigforss och näringslivet". *Stockholms-Tidningen*, November 6, 1938.

Ohlin, B. "Mobiliserings- och krigsekonomi". *Stockholms-Tidningen*, May 17, 1939.

Salter, A. *Planhushållning*. Stockholm: Tiden, 1934.

Salter, A., J. Stamp, J. M. Keynes, B. Blackett, H. Clay, and W. H. Beveridge. *The World's Economic Crisis and the Way of Escape*. London: George Allen and Unwin, 1931.

Schivelbusch, W. *Three New Deals: Reflections on Roosevelt's America, Mussolini's Italy, and Hitler's Germany, 1933–1939*. New York: Picador, 2006.

Social-Demokraten. "Staten och friheten". *Social-Demokraten*, August 26, 1935.

Steiger, O. *Studien zur Entstehung der Neuen Wirtschaftslehre in Schweden: Eine Anti-Kritik*. Berlin: Duncker & Humblot, 1971.

Stockholms-Tidningen. "Professor Cassels framstöt". *Stockholms-Tidningen*, February 16, 1930.

Stockholms-Tidningen. "Liberal valstart i Bromma i går". *Stockholms-Tidningen*, September 7, 1932.

Sunt Förnuft. "Ekonomi och demokrati". *Sunt Förnuft* 13(9) (1933): 395–396.

Svenska Dagbladet. "Regeringen har ingenting lärt, ingenting glömt". *Svenska Dagbladet*, March 7, 1934.

Svenska Dagbladet. "Klasskamp mot folkgemenskap". *Svenska Dagbladet*, March 7, 1934.

Svenska Dagbladet. "Planhushållning ett fantasiens gyckelord". *Svenska Dagbladet*, March 28, 1934.

Svenska Dagbladet. "'Kapitalismen har gjort underverk'. Prof. Cassel gisslar skarpt planhushållningssvärmeriet". *Svenska Dagbladet*, April 18, 1934.

Svenska Dagbladet. "Handelskammarmötet dryftar näringspolitiken. Planhushållningen utdömes av professor G. Åkerman". *Svenska Dagbladet*, June 19, 1934.

Svenska Dagbladet. "Gustav Cassels livsgärning". *Svenska Dagbladet*, January 17, 1945.

Temin, P. "Soviet and Nazi Economic Planning in the 1930s". *Economic History Review* 44(4) (1991): 573–593.

Tre tal hållna vid den middag som ett antal kolleger och lärjungar gav för Eli F. Heckscher och hans anhöriga den 13 december 1944 på restaurangen Tre Kronor i Stockholm. Stockholm, 1945.

Undersökning rörande behovet av en utvidgning av bostadsstatistiken jämte vissa därmed förbundna bostadspolitiska frågor. Stockholm: Isaac Marcus Boktryckeri-Aktiebolag, 1933 (SOU 1933: 14).

Wadensjö, E. "The Committee on Unemployment and the Stockholm School". In *The Stockholm School of Economics Revisited*, edited by L. Jonung, 103–124. Cambridge: Cambridge University Press, 1991.

Wennås, O. "Bertil Ohlin om socialismen, liberalismen och folkpartiet". In *Liberal ideologi och politik 1934–1984*, 80–142. Falköping: AB Folk & samhälle, 1984.

Westin Silverstolpe, G. Välstånd och fattigdom. In *Vår egen tids historia 1880–1930*, vol. 5, edited by Y. Lorents. Stockholm: Bonniers, 1938.

Wickman, K. *Makroekonomisk planering – orsaker och utveckling*. Uppsala: Almqvist & Wiksell International, 1980.

Wigforss, E. "Engelsk liberalism". *Tiden* 20(2) (1928): 65–70.

Wigforss, E. "Professor Cassel och socialismen". *Tiden* 21(2) (1929): 65–78.

Wigforss, E. "Ryska femårsplanen". *Tiden* 23(1) (1931): 18–26.

Wigforss, E. "Pånyttfödd kapitalism?" *Tiden* 24(5) (1932): 265–272.

Wigforss, E. "Ideologiska linjer i praktisk politik". *Tiden* 59(9) (1967): 525–533.

5

Summary and Conclusions

Abstract In this final chapter, the debate on economic planning is summarized, the advocates' and opponents' main arguments are reviewed and a number of questions are addressed: Which were the main foreign sources of inspiration? Swedish economists seldom referred to any sources of inspiration. Bertil Ohlin was the exception and his sources were mainly British. How did the economists affect Swedish economic policy? Gustav Cassel, Eli Heckscher and Ohlin exerted influence through their intense hammering out of arguments in leading newspapers while Gunnar Myrdal and Gösta Bagge were more involved in policy-making; Ohlin's "middle way" seems to have been particularly influential in the long run. How do the arguments of the Swedish economists compare to arguments of international heavyweights like Friedrich von Hayek and E. F. M. Durbin? The Swedish economists seem to have been at least as eminent in producing arguments for and against economic planning as their foreign colleagues. What can we today learn from the debate? Populist and nationalist regimes have a tendency to resort to violent government

© The Author(s) 2018   **137**
B. Carlson, *Swedish Economists in the 1930s Debate
on Economic Planning*, Palgrave Studies in Economic History,
https://doi.org/10.1007/978-3-030-03700-0_5

interventions to try to enhance their political and economic power and then the question arises, just as in the 1930s, how liberal market economies should respond. In this context, yesterday's arguments for and against economic planning have a more or less timeless actuality.

Keywords Economic planning · Arguments · Sources of inspiration · Influence · Actuality

In this final chapter, the debate on economic planning, as it has been depicted in Chapter 4, will be summarized, the main arguments will be reviewed, and the following questions will be addressed: Which were the main foreign sources of inspiration? How did the economists affect Swedish economic policy in the 1930s and in the longer run? How do the arguments of the Swedish economists compare to the arguments of a planning opponent like Friedrich von Hayek and a planning advocate like E. F. M. Durbin? What can we today learn from the debate?

Summary of the Debate

During the 1920s, the Swedish debate on the role of the state in the economy was lively and sometimes the term economic planning appeared. The debate was fuelled by experiences from World War I, the Bolshevik revolution in Russia, the advancing Social Democracy, structural unemployment and new ideas launched by British Liberals, among them John Maynard Keynes.

In the mid-1920s, Bertil Ohlin was intrigued by ideas of a "new (liberal) socialism" in Britain, whereas Eli Heckscher and Gustav Cassel opposed planning in their fight against socialism and communism. Heckscher appeared as a full-fledged market liberal in 1921 and got some unique insights into communist planning during a visit to Russia in 1925. He dismissed the old socialist view of capitalism as anarchic and found that the Russian planning authority, Gosplan, gave an impression of planlessness. He was not surprised. An ever so eminent expertise could not handle the "interplay between the thousands of forces which in combination shape the economic context".[1] Free price formation was the real expert. He warned against communist and fascist threats against spiritual freedom and the rule of law. Cassel touched upon much the same issues in 1926: the socialist accusation that capitalist production is anarchic and the liberal convictions that an economic top management can never manage such planning, that planning is not compatible with free choice of occupation and independent trade unions, that politicians are not suited to be economic managers. He also, just like Heckscher, invoked the Russian example as a planning failure.

In 1927, Ohlin took a forceful stand for economic planning. Economic conditions had changed due to the growth of large-scale corporations managed by salaried officials and due to long-term unemployment. "A planned organization, guaranteeing rationality and efficiency, instead of the laissez-faire system of the old society, has become the order of the day".[2] Rationality was more important than freedom. Liberalism must choose. There could be no compromise between the old market liberalism and the new social liberalism.

In 1928, Heckscher, Ernst Wigforss and Ohlin reacted to the "Yellow Book". Heckscher referred to his impressions from Russia, demanded that government and market performance be measured on similar scales, and warned that bureaucracy would put a "brake on the wheel" and that the interest of consumers would be "out of the picture".[3] Wigforss and Ohlin found the ideas of the British Liberals inspiring. Ohlin, however, cautioned against the conclusion that the solution was to completely abandon the existing system and put communism or socialism in its place. At the end of 1929, Cassel took the crash on Wall Street as a warning example of what happens when the state cannot manage one of its basic tasks, the care of the monetary system.

---

[1] E. Heckscher, "Intryck från Ryssland VI: 'Planhushållning' och förnöjsamhet", *Dagens Nyheter*, October 9, 1925.

[2] B. Ohlin, "Liberalismen vid skiljovägen", *Stockholms-Tidningen*, December 27, 1927.

[3] E. Heckscher, "Den icke-socialistiska framtidsstaten", *Dagens Nyheter*, February 17, 1928.

The fight over economic planning seems to have begun in earnest in 1930, when the Conservative government introduced a "milling obligation" which Heckscher branded as "economic planning with no plan, after the pattern familiar in Soviet Russia".[4] In Russia, the famous five-year plan suppressed consumption in order to promote large-scale capital formation. In fascist Italy, freedom of the press was gone.

In a 1931 discussion, Heckscher condemned the milling obligation for being worse than Russian planning since the Russians at least had some idea of what they wanted to achieve—"to pursue economic planning without a plan" was "just a little too absurd".[5] Johan Åkerman also aired his doubts about the Russian five-year plan. To decide how things would turn out in five or ten years was not feasible. A centralized, collectivist society set on planning would have to suppress unplanned inventions and regulate consumption and would thereby sacrifice progress. Cassel kept on blaming governments for the unfolding crisis. The free market economy had not been allowed to work according to its own laws. The price formation process, the core of capitalist society, had been brushed aside by the war, the peace treaty, nationalism, tariffs, subsidies, taxes and deflationary policies.

As Leif Lewin has demonstrated, Wigforss loosened the ties between socialization and planning at the Social Democratic congress of 1932.[6] The new ideology was vague, aiming for a more general government control over economic life. This vagueness was demonstrated when Gunnar Myrdal made his entry as an advocate of economic planning. He wrote of an idea "which creeps in everywhere" but is "a very undetermined thing".[7] Wigforss and Ohlin reviewed Arthur Salter's *Recovery*. Wigforss figured the book was not alien to the socialist movement. Ohlin found a masterly programme for liberalism's retreat to stronger positions. He, however, warned that state socialism would strengthen national antagonisms and in one respect sided with

---

[4]E. Heckscher, "Inmalningstvånget och dess konsekvenser", *Dagens Nyheter*, May 28, 1930.

[5]Nationalekonomiska Föreningen, "Inmalningen och vår spannmålspolitik", March 23, 1931, 51.

[6]L. Lewin, *Planhushållningsdebatten* (Stockholm: Almqvist & Wiksell, 1967).

[7]G. Myrdal, "Socialpolitikens dilemma II", *Spektrum* 2(4) (1932): 30.

Cassel (without mentioning him)—the world economic crisis was not the bankruptcy of the capitalist system but the bankruptcy of war and nationalism.

In the 1932 debate on public works in the Economic Society—the works programme was to be implemented by the Social Democratic government the following year—Gösta Bagge and Heckscher called for guarantees that the programme be terminated in boom periods. Heckscher thought that this programme would be more difficult to carry out than the Russian five-year plans, since these plans had a time frame, whereas the programme must be adapted to a business cycle unknown in advance, an argument which caused Ohlin to hit the ceiling.

When Heckscher in 1933 discussed dictatorship and technology, he outlined how organization, large units and control over communications had strengthened state power and bolstered Bolshevik–fascist–Nazi tendencies and he urged his fellow countrymen to defend Sweden against these evils. Ohlin insisted that new circumstances require new solutions and that economic planning was compatible with a liberal attitude.

The New Deal caught the attention in mid-1933. Ohlin argued that Franklin Roosevelt's plan was to create "a social-capitalist order as far from Manchester liberal capitalism as possible".[8] The alternative would have been a communist revolution. The *laissez-faire* of the late nineteenth century had been an exception, followed by tendencies of large-scale production, monopoly, business cycles, and agricultural overproduction. Economic policy must be adapted to these new conditions. Ohlin hinted at his idea of framework planning: "One must create an elastic frame, within which private initiatives and associations can shape a reasonably planned development".[9] Cassel was dismayed by Roosevelt's violent interventions and predicted that the experiment would fail. Nonetheless, the catchword of economic planning seemed to

---

[8]B. Ohlin, "Amerikas experiment: Det är med prisstegring som med vin: verkan beror på kvantiteten", *Stockholms-Tidningen*, July 20, 1933.

[9]B. Ohlin, "Organisation och anpassning", *Stockholms-Tidningen*, August 13, 1933.

exercise "an almost hypnotic effect" on the masses.[10] One intervention would lead to another in a never-ending sequence so that no equilibrium could ever be reached. To Ohlin, the problem was rather to get the ignorant masses to accept that some problems were so complicated that they must be solved by experts (planners).

In early 1934, when the Social Democrats revealed their intention to increase the influence of the state over economic life in spite of the economic recovery, the planning debate went into high gear. Myrdal opened the year with a report on the effects of fiscal policy in which he concluded that no "pure" market price had ever existed. One could change the course of price formation as one wished through a planned arrangement of the regulatory frame and long-term planning was a necessary precondition for a rational adaptation to changing circumstances. Cassel concluded that one had to be blind not to see that economic planning would lead to dictatorship irrespective of whether the underlying ideology was Bolshevism, fascism, Nazism or Rooseveltism.

When Myrdal succeeded Cassel as professor of economics at Stockholm University he gave a speech in which he claimed that central economic planning was not a choice but a necessity. The increasing volume of state interventions did not emanate from any quest for planning; it was the other way around. He explained how the liberal society differed from contemporary society. The former had had a stable frame of institutions within which small and mobile economic units could operate. The latter had a less stable frame within which bigger and less mobile units operated; they could now themselves design the rules of the game. Consequently, the state had to intervene. Myrdal clearly had his predecessor in mind when he talked of market liberalism as "an outdated utopia nourished by occasional untimely social dreamers".[11] Cassel responded that free price formation is a means to force different interests (producers, consumers) to make the concessions needed to achieve economic equilibrium. He ridiculed planners

---

[10]G. Cassel, "Staten och näringslivet", *Sunt Förnuft* 13(December) (1933): 399.
[11]G. Myrdal, "Installationsföreläsning den 31 mars 1934", in *Samhällskrisen och socialvetenskaperna* (Stockholm: Kooperativa förbundets bokförlag, 1935), 37.

for wanting to root out capitalism at the same time as they imagined there would always be private capital to seize. He found it paradoxical that communist Russia accumulated capital while capitalist America brushed capital aside.

Bagge, in two speeches in March 1934, complained that the concept of planning was elusive, even like a chameleon. He argued that trade union demands would lead to labour market sclerosis and economic planning. At the same time, he noted that in Russia, Germany and Italy, economic planning had resulted in dictatorship in the labour market. These regimes were characterized by *"planless command economy"* and the US was exposed to grotesquely planless policies.[12] He stressed that the decisive factor is the spirit in which government interventions are carried out. Conservative policy should be built upon experience and not upon (socialist) blueprints.

In April 1934, Cassel gave a major address on planning before the Federation of Swedish Industries. Just as Bagge, he reacted against blueprints of ideal societies of a kind which had been cultivated by "speculative spirits" since the days of Plato.[13] He advised planning enthusiasts to study the history of mercantilism and worried that planning ideas had crept into the bourgeois world. Planning had become a fashion. It was, however, not difficult to find examples of planning failures. In the Soviet Union, industries were built without taking transportation and distribution into consideration. In the US, sowing was subsidized at the same time as crops were destroyed. Planners tried to address these failures by collecting all powers in one hand, which resulted in dictatorship. But not even dictatorships could control a constantly changing reality. Things would go too far before the leadership perceived the need to change course and even farther before any measures were implemented. The following month, in his Cobden Lecture in London, Cassel depicted "a bewildering mass of government interferences of a steadily cumulative nature" which created demand for coordination:

---

[12]G. Bagge, *Svensk konservatism och tidslägets krav: Fyra föredrag* (Södertälje: Axlings Bok- och Tidskriftstryckeri, 1934), 36.

[13]G. Cassel, *"Planhushållning" Diskussion med inledningsföredrag av professor Gustav Cassel vid Sveriges Industriförbunds årsmöte den 17 April 1934* (Stockholm, 1934), 3.

"For this reason Planned Economy will always tend to develop into Dictatorship".[14] Once economic dictatorship was established, it would suffocate personal freedom, freedom of thought and expression and the independence of science. In an article in an American banking journal, Cassel depicted the vicious circle of planning. Monetary disorder (deflation) leads to demands for protectionism which leads to domestic interventions which leads to a need for coordination which leads to central planning. The great paradox was that governments which had not been able to stabilize the monetary system were now expected to stabilize the entire economy. Since progress (growth) implies disturbances, Cassel figured that planners implicitly assumed a static economy. To sacrifice progress to achieve stability was, however, "a tremendous price" for humanity to pay.[15]

Heckscher elaborated on the long perspective with mercantilism as a starting point and argued that under central planning, there might be fewer but more serious mistakes. Gustaf Åkerman portrayed economic planning as inflexible and hostile towards freedom and development. Cassel blasted dictatorships of all colours. Their economic ignorance was demonstrated when militaries were assigned to control price formation, "the finest regulator of economic life".[16] He particularly condemned Nazism as a denial of fundamental values in any culture of higher standing and a threat against freedom and the rule of law.

In late 1934, Heckscher's great showdown with economic planning took place at the Economic Society. He talked, just like Bagge, of planless command economy, attacked his younger colleagues as "apostles of the planned economy" and outlined a series of developments which had created an unprecedented scope for state direction—large-scale production, closed geographical frontiers, stationary population and modern "distributary systems" (natural monopolies); humanity had been woven into a network controlled from central points. This state direction was

---

[14]G. Cassel, "From Protectionism Through Planned Economy to Dictatorship", *International Conciliation*. Documents for the year 1934. New York (1934): 323

[15]G. Cassel, "Planned Economy", *American Bankers Association Journal* 26(July) (1934): 15.

[16]G. Cassel, "Sverige och diktaturerna", *Svenska Dagbladet*, November 14, 1934.

a threat to technological development, democracy and personal and spiritual freedom. Myrdal objected that Heckscher's "horrifying depiction" had nothing to do with planning. Economic planning was a yet not implemented ambition to increase economic mobility and adjustment in a way liberal economy had failed to do. Ohlin also accused Heckscher of having painted "an extreme picture of some sort of mystical, extreme command economy".[17] The liberal nineteenth-century order was outdated and the organizational apparatus had to be adapted to new conditions. He wished to discuss different types of public sector activities and not a cliché like economic planning. Ohlin particularly stressed the need for framework planning and dismissed any imminent danger of dictatorship. Heckscher was surprised that Myrdal and Ohlin had shied away from a discussion of principles and he, just as Bagge before him, emphasized that the spirit underlying interventions—socialism—was crucial. Myrdal and Ohlin argued that interventions must be made in time to defuse a crisis and avoid major dangers. When Heckscher published an extended version of his address, he added a further effect of planning: Economic planners turn into economic nationalists and every business transaction turns into a political act.

The last battle of 1934 was fought over Gunnar and Alva Myrdal's book on the population issue. Cassel accused the Myrdal's of using this issue to promote a communist society and Heckscher and his wife characterized the book as a crowbar with which to turn Swedish society upside down. The Myrdals replied that Cassel was empty-handed before the problem and that the Heckschers pursued cheap counterfeiting. Ohlin once more saw liberalism at the crossroads. Now, when the crisis was over, the choice was between state socialism and social liberalism.

Cassel in 1935 indicated three ways in which economic planning would destroy democracy. The democratic process was too slow to be able to guide the economy, the economy was so complicated that the parliament would be overstrained and compromises in parliament would result in inconsistent decisions. Those who wished to implement a planned economy must therefore be prepared to sacrifice the

---

[17]Nationalekonomiska Föreningen, "Planhushållning", November 20, 1934, 145–146, 151, 167, 185.

parliamentary and democratic system. Cassel, however, had an alternative to suggest, an economic council which could analyse economic problems and express its opinion, and which the government must listen to before submitting its proposals to the *Riksdag*.

The next major battle over planning took place when economists from the Nordic countries in 1935 convened in Oslo. Norwegian economist Wilhelm Keilhau gave the introduction and took the same stance as Heckscher had done in Stockholm the year before. He wished to discuss principles and not individual policy interventions. Keilhau delivered arguments similar to those presented by Heckscher and Cassel in Sweden. Ohlin claimed not to understand the notion of a totally planned economy. He insisted that organizational modes must be adapted to contemporary tendencies, such as large-scale production, new means of communication and reduced opportunities for migration, and threw out a forceful accusation: "It is Manchester liberal diehards, opposing all state interventions, who prepare the ground for dictatorship and communism".[18] Heckscher now referred to new tendencies, conducive to small-scale production and increased mobility, which meant that planned economy was an outdated phenomenon. Karin Kock intervened to defend Roosevelt's policies—to imagine that America was heading towards state socialism was to see ghosts in broad daylight. The battle of Oslo resulted in an exchange of letters in which Heckscher labelled Ohlin a Social Democrat and Ohlin labelled Heckscher a Conservative.

Ohlin expressed his satisfaction over the British "Next Five Years" plan with its aim to achieve a rational coordination of interventions already in place and the establishment of an economic general staff. This was social liberalism of his own taste. Cassel used Marxist historical materialism as a weapon against Social Democrats: Personal and intellectual freedom had been built on economic freedom and would be destroyed by a bureaucratic command economy.

---

[18]*Forhandlinger ved det tiende nordiske nasjonaløkonomiske møte i Oslo den 17-19 juni 1935.* "Kritisk vurdering av planøkonomien" (Oslo: Grøndahl & Søns Boktrykkeri, 1935), 38.

Heckscher in a 1936 address/paper dug into the relations between the world war and economic planning. The war had strengthened private monopoly, involved industrialists in economic controls and given birth to violent nationalism. However, the rise of command economy in the early 1930s had been so sudden that it must be explained as a change of mind: when the 1930s crisis erupted, the prosperity era of the 1920s had been perceived as "a devil's delusion" creating "a crisis of faith in the private economy".[19] Ohlin objected when the Prime Minister in a radio speech promised continued government control and better management of economic life. Could controllers really manage the economy better than business leaders? Cassel devoted himself to Marxism-bashing. The infatuation with economic planning was of Marxist origin and was focused on producer interests. A central organ could never design a satisfactory plan for a nation's economy and a state-planned economy could never adapt to the continually shifting conditions of economic life.

Ohlin now summarized his ideas in a book on "Free or Directed Economy". He outlined the structural transformation, with increased scale of production and decreased mobility, and the parallel transition from merchant to engineer mentality. He criticized *laissez-faire* and socialism and pleaded for social liberalism. He criticized the Social Democrats for not realizing that too much state intervention would entail overworked authorities, corruption and interest group conflicts. Supermen able to direct the whole economy simply did not exist. At the same time, he stated that government interventions in recent years had not been arbitrary but adapted to new circumstances. They had, however, been rather improvised and had to be coordinated. At the top of Ohlin's agenda was the institutional frame, "the fixed rules of the game", which allows the game to play out "with less friction and more efficiency".[20] He noted, as Myrdal before him, that the frame in the 19th liberal society had to a large extent been made up of informal constraints (conventions and traditions) and that over time there had been

---

[19]E. Heckscher, "Det privata näringslivet i tvångshushållningens tid", *Föredrag hållna inför svenska ekonomföreningen*, no. 1 (Stockholm, 1936), 12–13.

[20]B. Ohlin, *Fri eller dirigerad ekonomi* (Stockholm: Studieledningen för Folkpartiets Ungdomsförbund, 1936), 111.

a shift towards formal constraints. He also advocated economic policy with a longer time horizon. And, finally, he declared that freedom of thought and expression must never be limited, even if a dictatorship would be able to offer material gains. Heckscher, in his review of Ohlin's book, expressed relief that Ohlin had made an honest attempt to mark his own line and not exposed socialism under liberal flag. Sven Brisman thought it natural to apply the brake rather than the accelerator when the idea of planning spread across the world like an epidemic.

When Keynes' *General Theory* entered the stage, the oldest active Swedish economist, David Davidson, invoked Russia as a deterrent experiment. He wholeheartedly recommended "the Swedish experiment", with public works in times of crisis. Cassel and Heckscher reacted by claiming that Keynes' theory was all but general since it was based on the stagnant interwar economy. Ohlin reacted by attempting to establish in the face of the world that the younger generation of Stockholm economists had attacked the same set of problems as Keynes independently of him.

In 1939, confronted with the threat or war, Cassel and Heckscher were the ones demanding planning. Cassel called for a "master plan" for the transition from peace to war economy and Heckscher noted that economic planning "has its greatest task in a war situation and is probably the creation of it".[21] Now Ohlin was the less resolute actor. When the war broke out, Cassel complained about confusion and chaos: "Where is, behind all this, a guiding hand?"[22]

The Evolution of Arguments

After the death of Knut Wicksell in 1926, Gustav Cassel and Eli Heckscher were Sweden's most well-known and influential economists. They were both market liberals and active moulders of public opinion. They mobilized arguments against economic planning already in the

---

[21]Nationalekonomiska Föreningen, "Sveriges ekonomi inför världsläget", May 16, 1939, 103.
[22]G. Cassel, "Planlöshet och förmynderskap", *Svenska Dagbladet*, November 19, 1939.

mid-1920s, when they perceived threats from Swedish Social Democracy, Soviet communism and Italian fascism. Their arguments are of enduring quality, a claim to be substantiated below: The market economy is not anarchic, no central planner can master the enormous amount of information handled by the invisible hand (free price formation), politicians are not suited to be economic managers, bureaucracy is "a brake on the wheel", central planners cannot tolerate workers free choice of occupation, trade unions or consumers free choice of goods, planning experiments (Russia) exhibit planlessness and governments cannot even handle some of their most basic tasks in a market economy. Heckscher already in 1928 anticipated one of the major public choice arguments: One cannot assign a perfect theoretical state to correct imperfections in a real market; i.e., in the real world, there are both market and government failures.[23] Cassel was nourishing a similar idea when he dismissed the belief in the absolute rationality and effectiveness of state government.

A common perception is that Gunnar Myrdal, alongside Ernst Wigforss, was the chief instigator of economic planning ideas in Sweden. However, Bertil Ohlin began his attacks on market liberalism several years before Myrdal appeared on the planning stage. As has been established by Karl-Gustav Landgren, Ohlin followed the doings of British Liberals in general and John Maynard Keynes in particular.[24] The basic argument for planning was quite simple: there must be more economic rationality and efficiency.

Heckscher ignited the debate on economic planning in 1930 through his attacks on the milling obligation, which he compared to Soviet style planning or something even worse: planning without a plan. As the debate went into higher gear, the planning advocates Myrdal and Ohlin elaborated their set of arguments. They could not understand the picture painted by opponents "of some sort of mystical, extreme command economy"

---

[23]Wickman notes that Heckscher was a precursor of public choice thinking when arguing that politicians act partly out of self-interest. See K. Wickman, "Eli Heckscher – pionjär utan efterföljare", in E. Heckscher, *Om staten, liberalismen och den ekonomiska politiken: Texter i urval av Kurt Wickman* (Stockholm: Timbro, 2000).

[24]K.-G. Landgren, *Den'nya ekonomien' i Sverige: J.M. Keynes, E. Wigforss, B. Ohlin och utvecklingen 1927–1939* (Stockholm: Almqvist & Wiksell, 1960).

which would lead to dictatorship. Planning was, to quote Myrdal, a "very undetermined thing". Economic conditions had changed, mostly through larger economic units and an accompanying engineering mentality, which necessitated a new policy framework, new institutions. The economic crisis had necessitated a host of government interventions—the alternative would have been revolution and dictatorship—and these interventions must be coordinated in a rational and efficient way.

The opponents to planning also expanded their set of arguments: Policies should be based on experience and not on blueprints (particularly not socialist blueprints), planners will prioritize producer interests, the government will be overstrained, a planning authority will not be able to react fast enough in the face of changing circumstances, there will perhaps be fewer but much bigger mistakes, nationalist planning means that every business transaction becomes a political act. From 1933 and onwards, they could add two new examples to their set of scarecrows: Nazi Germany and New Deal USA.

Advocates and opponents shared some basic understandings. Economic conditions—the size of economic units and the dynamics of the world economy—as well as popular mentality had changed. However, they completely disagreed on how to tackle these changes. The advocates wished for a new rational and long-term framework. The opponents wished to retain as much leeway for market forces as possible since they did not regard them as outdated but rather well suited to drive the continuous economic transformation. Both sides acknowledged that government interventions must be coordinated. However, advocates wished for more and opponents for less intervention. The advocates wished to solve a range of specific problems. The opponents figured that each intervention would cause another in a cumulative process leading to dictatorship and the end of "spiritual" freedom.[25] Both sides wished to defend democracy but again disagreed on the means. The advocates believed that democracies had to use very much the same

---

[25]Interestingly, Myrdal is the Swedish economist most associated with cumulative processes, building on Wicksell. However, in the planning debate, it was rather his opponents who used the cumulative argument.

means as dictatorships to be able to compete with these, the opponents were convinced that the foundation of liberal democracies—the market economy—must be protected. The advocates had perhaps the upper hand in their analysis of changing economic conditions, but they hesitated to discuss principles. They wished to discuss reasonable interventions but the consequence when all interventions were to be coordinated was seen as a thing of the future. In this attitude, the kinship between socialism and planning can be seen: sharp criticism of current conditions but reluctance to discuss what an alternative model would entail. The opponents wished to discuss principles. They wished to debate what a fully developed command economy would look like and they could use communist, fascist and Nazi examples to substantiate their dystopia.

Ohlin's "Free or Directed Economy" in 1936 rounded off the debate on planning and laid out a middle way; "a clever act of balance in the inflamed debate on economic planning", according to his biographer Sven-Erik Larsson.[26] Ohlin had been the leading planning advocate among economists early on and he had been tough on his mentors Heckscher and Cassel. He had, however, always, unlike Myrdal, drawn a borderline against socialism. Like Keynes, he wished to save essential elements of the competitive market economy, and, as the economy recovered, the liberal traits of his social liberalism grew stronger. Ohlin anticipated the new institutional economics when he explained that institutions make out "the rules of the game" in order to reduce friction (transaction costs). Myrdal had expressed similar thoughts in his 1934 inaugural lecture.

Sources of Inspiration

The Swedish economists seldom referred to any sources of inspiration. Ohlin was the exception and his sources were mainly British: Lloyd George's Liberals, Keynes, Salter, Blackett, the "Next Five Years" plan. How the others procured their ideas is more or less obscure. This is not very surprising since their arguments were mostly put forward in

---

[26]S.-E. Larsson, *Bertil Ohlin* (Stockholm: Atlantis, 1996), 146.

public debates and newspapers. In the case of Cassel and Myrdal, it is even less astonishing. They were both, mentor as well as revolting mentee, particular about appearing as the very originators of most of their ideas. Bagge, with inspiration from a Norwegian politician, said that economic planning required mass or serf mentality, which is somewhat interesting in view of the title of Hayek's 1944 book: *The Road to Serfdom*.

One question, which can hardly be answered, is if the opponents to planning were aware of the early socialist calculation debate. In any case, they did not, except for Davidson, refer to Mises or Hayek. One should bear in mind that Cassel (born 1866) and Heckscher (born 1879) were both older than Mises (born 1881) and much older than Hayek (born 1899). The Swedes had fought socialism since the turn of the century 1900 and probably did not experience any imminent need to import arguments from younger colleagues in other countries. Cassel was notorious for being sparing in his use of references. On the other hand, in his memoirs, most people of any importance he had interacted with are mentioned. Mises and Hayek are not among them. Heckscher exchanged a few letters with Hayek, but only after the Second World War (concerning the Mont Pelerin Society).

Influence on Economic Policy

A (hopeless) question, which has already been somewhat touched upon, concerns the influence of the economists on Swedish economic policy in the 1930s and in the longer run. As stated in the introduction, the ambition of the present book has not been to try to follow the line of economists' arguments into the political sphere of arguing and decision-making. We have to settle for some general remarks. Cassel, Heckscher and Ohlin undoubtedly exerted influence on the public opinion through their intense hammering out of arguments in leading newspapers. At least the younger generation of economists underlined how the older one had dominated in the 1920s. Ohlin found that the opinion in politico-economic issues in those days was influenced primarily by Cassel's and Heckscher's newspaper articles and discussions in the Economic Society,[27] and Erik Lundberg considered that Cassel and Wicksell had the greatest influence on opinions and policies, followed by Heckscher.[28] Wigforss even regarded Heckscher as a "navigation mark" for anyone sailing the politico-economic seas since he represented a coherent liberal ideology which a socialist could not just bypass.[29] Bagge eventually (from 1935) exerted his influence as leader of the Conservative Party. The older generation was just as active in the 1930s, but was challenged by the younger. Myrdal exerted his influence as a "social engineer" involved in Social Democratic policy-making and Timothy Tilton concludes that "there can be no doubt about Myrdal's impact upon Swedish social and economic policy; wherever one looks – family policy, countercyclical policy and economic planning, housing, the school system, agriculture, sexual enlightenment, women's issues – his impact is visible".[30] Ohlin was, as we have seen, a planning advocate early on, but at the same time, a guardian against far-reaching state socialism. Later on, as leader of the Liberal Party, he led the opposition against Social Democracy for many years. "His brand of liberalism was influential in the Swedish post-World War II period, making the policies of the ruling Social Democrats less socialistic".[31] Sweden was dubbed "the middle way" already in the 1930s and the question is if Ohlin's 1936 guidepost is not one of the best indicators of what was to come.

Anyway, when Sweden's first long-term programme—or four-year plan—was designed in 1948, it was not on the initiative of Myrdal or the Social Democrats, but on the demand of OEEC directed to the countries involved in the Marshall Plan. The brain behind this

---

[27]Heckscher was, as we have seen, a dominating force in the Economic Society, but Cassel had withdrawn from this forum already in 1920. See B. Ohlin, "Några intryck från Nationalekonomiska föreningen 1918–23", in *Ekonomisk debatt och ekonomisk politik: Nationalekonomiska föreningen 100 år*, ed. J. Herin and L. Werin (Stockholm: Norstedts, 1977).

[28]E. Lundberg, *Kriserna och ekonomerna* (Malmö: LiberFörlag, 1984).

[29]E. Wigforss, *Minnen II: 1914–1932* (Stockholm: Tidens Förlag, 1951), 55.

[30]T. Tilton, "Gunnar Myrdal and the Swedish Model", in *Gunnar Myrdal and His Works*, ed. G. Dostaler, D. Ethier, and L. Lepage (Montreal: Harvest House Ltd, 1992), 36.

[31]R. Findlay, L. Jonung, and M. Lundahl (eds.), *Bertil Ohlin: A Centennial Celebration (1899–1999)* (Cambridge, MA: MIT Press, 2002), 5.

programme and several following ones was Ingvar Svennilson, who had for several years headed a business think tank, the Industrial Institute of Economic and Social Research (*Industriens Utredningsinstitut*). Svennilson did not portray his creation as a plan like those in the outspoken planning countries but as a relatively uncertain estimate of the future.[32] In the mid-1960s, he outlined the aim of Sweden's long-term planning as follows:

> Price formation should be used as a steering instrument to replace rationing according to certain criteria or brought about through queuing. The implications of this view are that one accepts the consumer's perception of what is best for him and rejects the idea of government "guardianship" in respect to consumer's choice.[33]

Cassel, Heckscher and Bagge must have drawn a sigh of relief in their heaven.

A Comparison with Hayek and Durbin

To what extent did the Swedish economists deliver arguments of more enduring relevance? I will limit myself to compare some of the main arguments distilled from the Swedish debate with the most influential body of arguments against planned economy ever presented, Hayek's *The Road to Serfdom* (1944),[34] and to counter-arguments delivered

---

[32]B. Carlson and M. Lundahl, "Ingvar Svennilson on Economic Planning in War and Peace", *History of Economic Ideas* 25(2) (2017).

[33]I. Svennilson, "Swedish Long-Term Planning—The Fifth Round", *Skandinaviska Banken Quarterly Review* 47(2) (1966): 38.

[34]A comparison could also be made between opponents and Mises' 1945 address, "Planning for Freedom", where he argues about the importance of market prices as the steering mechanism of the economy, capitalism as the system which serves the consumer best, the importance of capital accumulation for economic growth, the importance of sound monetary policy, government interventions as causes for the depression, etc.

by his critic E. F. M. Durbin.[35] Let us begin by comparing Swedish opponents' arguments to similar arguments in Hayek's book.[36]

- The market economy is not anarchic.

  [...] everybody who is not a complete fatalist is a planner. [...] An economist, whose task is the study of how men actually do act and how they might plan their affairs, is the last person who could object to planning in this general sense.[37]

- No central planner can master the enormous amount of information handled by the invisible hand (free price formation) and planning authorities are not able to react fast enough in the face of changing circumstances.

  And because all the details of the changes constantly affecting the conditions of demand and supply of the different commodities can never be fully known, or quickly enough be collected and disseminated, by any one center, what is required is some apparatus of registration which automatically records all the relevant effects of individual actions and whose indications are at the same time the result of, and the guide for, all the individual decisions. This is precisely what the price system does under competition, and which no other system promises to accomplish.[38]

- Bureaucracy is "a brake on the wheel".

---

[35]E. F. M. Durbin, *Problems of Economic Planning* (London: Routledge & Kegan Paul, 1949). We will use an article, "Professor Hayek on Economic Planning", originally published in *Economic Journal* 1945.

[36]The comparison will lean towards arguments *against* planning simply because the opponents, compared to the advocates, were more inclined to forge arguments of a principled character. Hayek, in his recommendations for further reading, included one Swedish contribution, G. Cassel, "From Protectionism through Planned Economy to Dictatorship".

[37]F. A. Hayek, *The Road to Serfdom* (London: G. Routledge & Sons Ltd, 1944), 34–35.

[38]Ibid., 49.

[...] the method of central direction is incredibly clumsy, primitive and limited in scope.[39]

- Central planners cannot tolerate workers free choice of occupation, trade unions or consumers free choice of goods.

  If they want to plan, they must control the entry into the different trades and occupations, or the terms of remuneration, or both. [—] And since the authority would have the power to thwart any efforts to elude its guidance, it would control what we consume almost as effectively as if it directly told us how to spend our income.[40]

- One intervention will cause another in a cumulative process leading to dictatorship and the end of "spiritual" freedom.

  [...] the close interdependence of all economic phenomena makes it difficult to stop planning just where we wish and [...], once the free working of the market is impeded beyond a certain degree, the planner will be forced to extend his controls until they become all-comprehensive. [—] Most planners who have seriously considered the political aspects of their task have little doubt that the directed economy must be run on more or less dictatorial lines. [—] It is because successful planning requires the creation of a common view on the essential values that the restrictions of our freedom with regard to material things touches so directly on our spiritual freedom.[41]

- Planners will prioritize producer interests.

  [...] an authority directing the whole economic system would be the most powerful monopolist conceivable.[42]

---

[39]Ibid., 50.
[40]Ibid., 94–95.
[41]Ibid., 88, 105, 113.
[42]Ibid., 93.

• Nationalist planning means that every economic transaction becomes a political act.

> [...] if international economic relations, instead of being relations between individuals, become increasingly relations between whole nations organized as trading bodies, they inevitably become the source of friction and envy between whole nations.[43]

• Wartime is the only time when a planned economy is necessary.

> The only exception to the rule that a free society must not be subjected to a single purpose is war and other temporary disasters when subordination of almost everything to the immediate and pressing need is the price at which we preserve our freedom in the long run.[44]

Some of the advocates' arguments can also be compared to Hayek's positions. Myrdal's view of planning as "a very undetermined thing" corresponds to Hayek's statement that the "idea of central economic planning owes its appeal largely to [the] very vagueness of its meaning".[45] The advocates' argument that technological change, with ever larger economic units, makes planning inevitable is dismissed by Hayek as one of the "familiar economic fallacies – the perceived necessity of the general growth of monopolies in consequence of technological developments".[46] The idea that planning arose out of an engineering mentality was not questioned by Hayek but he figured it was "fostered by the uncritical transfer to the problems of society of habits of thought engendered by the preoccupation with technological problems, the habits of thought of the natural scientist and the engineer".[47]

---

[43]Ibid., 220.
[44]Ibid., 206.
[45]Ibid., 34.
[46]Ibid., 188.
[47]Ibid., 20.

Now for some comparisons with Durbin's arguments. Myrdal envisioned economic planning as "a very undetermined thing". Durbin recalls his own statement from 1935: "Planning does not in the least imply the existence of a Plan". Planning in Durbin's sense means that economic decision-making is elevated from private businesses to representatives of the community—"we are speaking of a centralized administration". And, "if 'economic planning' involves no 'economic plan' in Professor Hayek's sense, then all his arguments against 'planning' fall to the ground". If Durbin scores here, it would mean that the opponents' ridicule of planless planning would similarly fall to the ground. The Swedish advocates questioned the picture of a "mystical, extreme command economy". Durbin in the same way questioned Hayek's picture of a "regimented and cruel society". The advocates did not see planning leading to dictatorship. Neither did Durbin: "We have a long tradition of increasing democracy combined with the growing activity of the State". The advocates argued that new economic conditions required a new policy framework, new institutions. Durbin emphasized the need to experiment with new institutions and held that "planning is likely to be a more efficient method of reaching any chosen set of ends because reason is superior to instinct and knowledge to ignorance".[48] Just as the Swedish opponents to planning, Hayek claimed that personal and political freedom had never existed without freedom in economic affairs. Durbin objected that this was to confuse cause and effect. The middle classes (in Britain) had first grasped political power and then secured economic freedom for themselves. However, if we are to believe Myrdal, this seemingly important issue of cause and effect is of no interest since the perception that economic freedom can be greater or lesser is a "metaphysic apriorism" in the heads of naïve market liberals.[49]

---

[48]Durbin, *Problems of Economic Planning*, 92, 95–97, 103. Durbin, however, did not care much for a perfectly competitive market: He saw such a market as an expression of a pre-rational and pre-scientific age and likened it to communities of ants and bees.

[49]Myrdal, "Installationsföreläsning den 31 mars 1934", 23.

All in all, it seems as if the Swedish economists were at least as eminent in producing arguments for and against economic planning as their foreign colleagues. We can thus confirm the conclusions (mentioned in the introduction) reached by Leif Lewin and Kurt Wickman.

Lessons for Our Time

Even though it is tempting to conjure up similarities between the 1930s and the 2010s, we have so far not in our time seen the rise of ruthless dictatorships and planning experiments like Soviet Russia and Nazi Germany but rather an emergence of populist and nationalist authoritarian regimes not particularly hostile to free markets as long as these do not (like the free press) challenge their authority. However, such regimes will always have a tendency to resort to violent government interventions to try to strengthen their political and economic power. And then the question arises, just like it did in the 1930s: should liberal market economies stick to their own paths or should they, to be "competitive", show more government muscles? What are the dangers of doing too little or doing too much? It is in this context that the arguments for and against economic planning of the 1930s (or, for that matter, the 1940s) have a more or less timeless actuality.

References

Bagge, G. *Svensk konservatism och tidslägets krav: Fyra föredrag*. Södertälje: Axlings Bok- och Tidskriftstryckeri, 1934.

Carlson, B., and M. Lundahl. "Ingvar Svennilson on Economic Planning in War and Peace". *History of Economic Ideas* 25(2) (2017): 115–138.

Cassel, G. "Staten och näringslivet". *Sunt Förnuft* 13(December) (1933): 397–399.

Cassel, G. *"Planhushållning" Diskussion med inledningsföredrag av professor Gustav Cassel vid Sveriges Industriförbunds årsmöte den 17 April 1934*, no. 2. Stockholm, 1934.

Cassel, G. "From Protectionism Through Planned Economy to Dictatorship". *International Conciliation*. Documents for the year 1934. New York (1934): 307–325.

Cassel, G. "Planned Economy". *American Bankers Association Journal* 26(July) (1934): 15–17, 49.

Cassel, G. "Sverige och diktaturerna". *Svenska Dagbladet*, November 14, 1934.

Cassel, G. "Planlöshet och förmynderskap". *Svenska Dagbladet*, November 19, 1939.

Durbin, E. F. M. *Problems of Economic Planning*. London: Routledge & Kegan Paul, 1949.

Findlay, R., L. Jonung, and M. Lundahl (eds.). *Bertil Ohlin: A Centennial Celebration (1899–1999)*. Cambridge, MA: MIT Press, 2002.

Forhandlinger ved det tiende nordiske nasjonaløkonomiske møte i Oslo den 17-19 juni 1935. "Kritisk vurdering av planøkonomien", 11–78. Oslo: Grøndahl & Søns Boktrykkeri, 1935.

Hayek, F. A. von. *The Road to Serfdom*. London: G. Routledge & Sons Ltd, 1944.

Heckscher, E. "Intryck från Ryssland VI: 'Planhushållning' och förnöjsamhet". *Dagens Nyheter*, October 9, 1925.

Heckscher, E. "Den icke-socialistiska framtidsstaten". *Dagens Nyheter*, February 17, 1928.

Heckscher, E. "Inmalningstvånget och dess konsekvenser". *Dagens Nyheter*, May 28, 1930.

Heckscher, E. "Det privata näringslivet i tvångshushållningens tid". *Föredrag hållna inför svenska ekonomföreningen*, no. 1. Stockholm, 1936.

Landgren, K.-G. *Den 'nya ekonomien' i Sverige: J.M. Keynes, E. Wigforss, B. Ohlin och utvecklingen 1927–1939*. Stockholm: Almqvist & Wiksell, 1960.

Larsson, S.-E. *Bertil Ohlin*. Stockholm: Atlantis, 1998.

Lewin, L. *Planhushållningsdebatten*. Stockholm: Almqvist & Wiksell, 1967.

Lundberg, E. *Kriserna och ekonomerna*. Malmö: LiberFörlag, 1984.

Mises, L. von. "Planning for Freedom". In *Economic Planning*, edited by L. von Mises and R. F. Tucker, 1–14. New York: Dynamic America, 1945.

Myrdal, G. "Socialpolitikens dilemma II". *Spektrum* 2(4) (1932): 13–31.

Myrdal, G. "Installationsföreläsning den 31 mars 1934". In *Samhällskrisen och socialvetenskaperna*, 7–41. Stockholm: Kooperativa förbundets bokförlag, 1935.

Nationalekonomiska Föreningen. "Inmalningen och vår spannmålspolitik", March 23, 1931.

Nationalekonomiska Föreningen. "Planhushållning", November 20, 1934.
Nationalekonomiska Föreningen. "Sveriges ekonomi inför världsläget", May 16, 1939.
Ohlin, B. "Liberalismen vid skiljovägen". *Stockholms-Tidningen*, December 27, 1927.
Ohlin, B. "Amerikas experiment: Det är med prisstegring som med vin: verkan beror på kvantiteten". *Stockholms-Tidningen*, July 20, 1933.
Ohlin, B. "Organisation och anpassning". *Stockholms-Tidningen*, August 13, 1933.
Ohlin, B. *Fri eller dirigerad ekonomi*. Stockholm: Studieledningen för Folkpartiets Ungdomsförbund, 1936.
Ohlin, B. "Några intryck från Nationalekonomiska föreningen 1918–23". In *Ekonomisk debatt och ekonomisk politik: Nationalekonomiska föreningen 100 år*, edited by J. Herin and L. Werin, 15–34. Stockholm: Norstedts, 1977.
Svennilson, I. "Swedish Long-Term Planning—The Fifth Round". *Skandinaviska Banken Quarterly Review* 47(2) (1966): 37–44.
Tilton, T. "Gunnar Myrdal and the Swedish Model". In *Gunnar Myrdal and His Works*, edited by G. Dostaler, D. Ethier, and L. Lepage, 13–36. Montreal: Harvest House Ltd, 1992.
Wickman, K. "Eli Heckscher—pionjär utan efterföljare". In Heckscher, E., *Om staten, liberalismen och den ekonomiska politiken: Texter i urval av Kurt Wickman*, 11–52. Stockholm: Timbro, 2000.
Wigforss, E. *Minnen II: 1914–1932*. Stockholm: Tidens Förlag, 1951.

Index

Printed by Printforce, the Netherlands